The National Tour of the USS Constitution 1931 – 1934

To Thank the Children and Patriotic Citizens

1931   1934

By

Lieutenant Commander Phillip K. Parker, USNR (Ret.)

Phillip K. Parker
April 10th, 2023

ISBN: 978-1-7923-0152-0
Library of Congress Control Number: 2019905043

COVER PHOTO:
Wintry Day in Boston, January 18, 2014, courtesy of U.S. Navy,
    Mass Communications, Specialist Second Class Peter Melkus

Photos in the book were provided by Phillip K. Parker, are in the public
domain, or the sources are credited.

For information please write to Phillip K. Parker
2333 Bonnevue Square, Billings, MT 59102
Phone: (406) 245-0659

This book is printed on acid-free paper.
Set in ITC Slimbach and Impact

Designed by Stacie French
French Impressions Graphic Design
safrench1@bresnan.net

Contents

A photo of the USS *Constitution* that was gifted to the author by a family member. The frigate was moored on the York River near York, Virginia, 1931.

Forward

MY INTEREST in the National Tour of Old Ironsides stems from the fact that a great uncle, Harry Moore, was a member of her crew. A Storekeeper First Class at the time, he also served as the ship's postal clerk. Around the time of Old Ironside's cruise, a group of hobbyists who collected naval postmarks organized into Universal Ship Cancellation Society, of which he was a member. Naturally, cancellations and covers from the *Constitution* were much sought after by these collectors. Writing in the September 1934 issue of the U. S. Naval Institute's *Proceedings*, another collector wrote:

> "No story about naval postmarks would be complete without mentioning the most famous postmark in the Navy. This item, in many different forms and dates, reposes in the album of every collector. I refer to the postmark of the historic U.S. Frigate *Constitution*. The Navy mail clerk on board, Harry Moore, SK1c, has been and always will be a true friend of the naval cover collection fraternity. I venture to say, without fear of contradiction, that Mr. Moore, with his cancelling device gripped in his sturdy right arm, has postmarked over 4,000,000 covers in the two years the frigate has been on tour. On one particular day, when the *Constitution* was at Seattle, Washington, he applied his postmark to over 1,600 covers!" [1]

Harold Moore enlisted in the Navy during World War I from Easthampton, Massachusetts, and had risen to the rank of Chief Petty Officer by the outbreak of World War II. During the war, he was commissioned as an officer and retired after the war as a Lieutenant, Supply Corps, U.S. Navy. I met him on two occasions, the first when I was eight years old and remembered mostly for the numerous sheltie dogs that populated the household. On the second occasion, I was a Second Class Midshipman with a few days leave before the start of summer training. I had decided to visit my great uncle in Massachusetts to see if I could tickle a few sea stories out of him. In this I was not disappointed, as memories rolled out of the old man in a magical afternoon at his Easthampton farm house.

Years later, I received some memorabilia from another uncle, consisting of a small beer mug from the Submarine Bar in the Panama Canal Zone, some postal covers and a weathered black and white photo in a plain wooden frame. The photo on page two is of the *Constitution* in full dress ship, with the funnel of the USS *Grebe* showing on the far side. The inscription on the reverse reads:

"The United States Frigate "Constitution" moored to a buoy in the York River — off Yorktown, Va.— Oct. 19, 1931. In full dress with the national ensign at the Fore and Main trucks.

"The battleship "Arkansas" in full dress with President's [Hon. Herbert Hoover's] Flag at the Fore-truck, lying astern. Occasion of the Sesqui-centennial celebration of surrender of Lord Cornwallis to General George Washington at Yorktown, Va. — Oct. 19, 1781.

"The U.S. Minesweeper *Grebe*, tender to the "Constitution" made fast along the starboard side.

"This picture framed on board the 'Constitution' by Charles Stewart, Seaman, at Washington, D.C., evening of 6 November, 1932.

"Harry Moore, Navy Mail Clerk, 'Old Ironsides,' 11/6/1932"

— *Phillip Parker, July 2018*

Harry Moore after he reached Chief Petty Officer Rank.

Secretary of Navy Charles Adams and Chief of Naval Operations Admiral William Pratt. *(Naval History and Heritage Command photo)*

USS *Constitution* in Dry Dock at the Boston Navy Yard for the 1927 Restoration. *(Naval History and Heritage Command photo)*

Chapter 1

The Restoration of 1927

ON JULY 2, 1931, THE VENERABLE United States Frigate *Constitution* left Boston on a three-year, goodwill tour that would make 90 stops, including 76 United States ports, cover 22,000 miles and entertain more than 4.6 million visitors to the ship. After completing a four-year restoration, financed in part by the pennies, nickels and dimes of school children, Secretary of the Navy Charles F. Adams started the tour with an invitation to those children and the rest of the nation:

"We hope," Secretary Adams stated, "that the children and patriotic citizens whose contributions made possible in a large degree the restoration of the famous ship will accept this invitation to board her. 'Old Ironsides' is more than an inspiration — she is an American tradition. The successful accomplishment of her mission at sea when she was commanded so ably by Hull, Bainbridge, and Stewart meant more to our young nation than the victories credited to her in the pages of history." [1]

So commenced a U. S. Navy public relations operation never matched before or since. The tour came at a good time. In circumstances unanticipated when the restoration was begun, the Great Depression was in its third year when it was completed. Americans needed something to feel good about and of which to be proud. The storied frigate, masts climbing skyward, was the perfect tonic for a beleaguered people.

At the end of the First World War, the *Constitution* was at the nadir of one of her periodic restoration and decay cycles. In February 1924, a survey of the ship was ordered to determine her future. Aware of the public's attachment to the ship, it was decided to restore her. The definitive reference on the ship, *A Most Fortunate Ship*, by Captain Tyrone G. Martin, USN, describes the restoration in some detail, to include the following list of defects noted before it commenced:

- Leakage requiring a tug to come alongside and pump her out daily
- Stern nearly totally decayed
- Port side bulged out nearly a foot more than the starboard side
- Stem skewed nine inches to port
- Fourteen and a half inch hogging (bending upward in the middle) in the hull
- Keelson broken aft of the foremast step
- Extensive wet and dry rot and concrete patching. [2]

The ship was not so much restored as it was re-built. The ship's prospective Commanding Officer for the tour, Commander Louis J. Gulliver, estimated that only fifteen percent of the original vessel remained. Writing in *Marine Review*, Gulliver offered, "The fifteen percent that remains contains, we feel sure, the soul of 'Ironsides'. That would be true if one percent of her remained and ninety-nine percent were new." [3]

The cost of the restoration was originally estimated at $473,725. Secretary of the Navy Curtis Wilbur, in 1924, asked Congress to authorize the restoration if the funds could be raised by private donations. He felt this would give the public a more direct connection to the beloved ship (and, no doubt, preserve funds for more modern needs). As anyone who has renovated an old house knows, the true cost of the project will not be known until the framework is exposed. By 1926, the estimated cost to complete had climbed to $650,654; up again to $747,983 when the bills for supplies started to come in; finally finishing at $987,000 (or about $14 million in 2016 dollars). Congress eventually chipped in about $300,000, the rest came from the national campaign to save the ship, including about $135,000 from school children.

The challenges faced by the restoration effort were gigantic. What drawings and data could be found were from different times in the ship's history. In the end, the 1925–1931 effort restored the ship to approximately her appearance in the 1850s. Authentic materials were hard to come by, especially live oak and the natural "knee" timbers that joined the decks to the hull. A long forgotten stash of 1,500 tons of live oak dating from the 1850s was found at the Pensacola Naval Air Station. Douglas Fir from Washington State was substituted for the original long leaf yellow pine deck planking. Fortunately, there remained on active duty one very able man who understood wooden ship construction—Naval Constructor Lieutenant John Abell Lord.

Lord was terrified that the old ship was so hogged and distorted that she would break in two when dry docked. He took elaborate measures to brace and support her before successfully easing her down onto the blocks of Dry Dock One, Boston Naval Shipyard, on June 16, 1927. Now the work could truly begin. As the frigate was reborn, only a few concessions to modernity were made. Lord installed a brig on the berth deck. Although none had been found in

Lieutenant John A. Lord on the spar deck, 1929.
(Naval History and Heritage Command photo)

his drawings, he figured there had to be one. Modern toilet facilities were provided in the old head area. A modern stove was provided in the galley along with new fresh water tanks and piping, a lighting system (available in port only), peloruses in the waist to aid in maneuvering, and a telephone on the quarter deck.

On July 1, 1931, the United States Frigate *Constitution* was recommissioned at Boston amid much pomp and ceremony. [4]

At the commissioning ceremony, the work of Lieutenant Lord was recognized by Rear Admiral Nulton, the Charleston Navy Yard Commander. The ceremony without Lord's presence, said the Admiral, "would be like Hamlet with Hamlet left out." A plaque honoring Lord's contribution was also placed above the spar deck. After writing a full report on the restoration effort, Lord retired with 34 years of Naval service. [5]

Commander Louis J. Gulliver, in full dress and fore and aft hat aboard the USS *Constitution*. *(Naval History and Heritage Command, photo NH49220)*

Chapter 2

The Captain—
Commander Louis J. Gulliver

LOUIS J. GULLIVER WAS BORN in Portland, Maine, in 1883. He attended both Yale and Cornell Universities for a year before attending the Naval Academy with the Class of 1907. On reporting his appointment to the Naval Academy, the *Portland Press* noted that he had "passed the mental examination with a very high rank," and that "He is tall and of an athletic build, of pleasant disposition and popular with all who know him." [1]

The 1907 Lucky Bag, the Naval Academy year book, had this to say about him: "The radius of his intellectual domain extends from Ithaca to New Haven and, after a sojourn in each of these universities, retrograded to Annapolis where he has obtained the distinction of Lord High Admiral of the Rhinos. Believes nothing unless he sees it in the New York Sun and asserts with a New England accent that 'Fellows should not study for marks.' Treats with scorn those who come beneath the palm of his displeasure, but a staunch friend of the baseball team and the greatest 'fan' in the brigade, thinks like a father, talks like a senator, but a problem unsolved, A poor mixer but a good fellow." [2]

"Rhino," in contemporary Naval Academy slang, was a chronic grumbler. So we have a picture of a cerebral, but not particularly sociable young man.

Another, if less credible, indication of his character was an analysis of his handwriting in the *Maine Sunday Telegram* after he assumed command of the *Constitution*:

> "The interesting specimen of handwriting for our consideration today, formed as it is of extravagant, defiant and unconventional pen strokes is expressive of great individuality, independence of opinion and fearlessness of spirit. This is the signature of Commander Louis J. Gulliver of the U. S. Navy and now in command of 'Old Ironsides'." [3]

Having read Commander Gulliver's Night Order Book, one can only say that his handwriting is neat and legible.

Following graduation, he had his first experience with a public relations operation when he sailed with Teddy Roosevelt's Great White Fleet around the world.

His career progressed normally until December 2, 1925, when disaster struck. The collier USS *Orion* (AC-11) with Lieutenant Commander Gulliver in command, went hard aground off Cape Henry, Virginia. The ship was heavily damaged along about 65 feet of the underwater hull and limped into port with a severe list to port. Because the Navy was shifting from coal to oil fuel and the extensive cost of repairs, the *Orion* was decommissioned and scrapped in 1926. [4]

That might have ended his career right there, but apparently he had a good enough record and possessed enough positive qualities that he was given another chance. He was promoted to Commander and assigned as Executive Officer to the old cruiser USS *Rochester* (CA-2). The "Rocky" was no plum assignment. She was a relic of the Old Steel Navy, originally commissioned as USS *New York* in 1893. In the late 1920s and early 1930s she was patrolling the Caribbean with a beefed up Marine detachment of about 200 men, part of the American gunboat diplomacy of that era.

So how was it that this obscure Commander with a blot on his record and serving a twilight tour on an antique warship became the Commanding Officer of the *Constitution* for her National Tour? He may have come to the attention of the higher-ups in the Navy Department through his gifted pen. He was a prolific author of articles and essays across a number of Naval and Merchant Marine related publications. His writing on technical and naval subjects is clear, concise and readable. An article he wrote for *Leatherneck,* the magazine of the Marine Corps Association, about how he recruited and employed a Marine Detachment for the *Constitution* is particularly entertaining. He was, by all accounts, an articulate and charming man. Also, Gulliver was apparently involved as an active volunteer in the National Campaign to save Old Ironsides. [5]

At the time of the National Tour, Gulliver was married with four children—Louis J. Gulliver Jr., then a midshipman at the Naval Academy, Grace, 19, Mary, 8 and Anne, 5.

Gulliver was known to the Superintendent of the Naval Academy, Admiral Thomas C. Hart and the Admiral sent him a personal letter, dated May 27, 1932. It said, in part, "I noted a Gulliver on the list of candidates and surmised that it was your son. As I recall, you set him quite a pace in your own Academic career and he has something cut out for himself if he equals or approaches that record." [6]

Sadly, the younger Gulliver was lost in action in the early days of World War II, when the gunboat USS *Ashville* was set upon by Japanese destroyers south of Java.

Commander Gulliver with President Hoover and Secretary of the Navy Charles F. Adams aboard the *Constitution*.
(Library of Congress photo)

Gulliver was ordered detached from the *Rochester* to command the *Constitution* on February 24, 1931. His orders include this statement: "The Secretary of the Navy has determined that this employment on shore duty is in the public interest." This sounds more like compliance with some congressional mandate to keep naval officers at sea where they belong instead of a statement of importance of the mission. [7] By the time he reached Boston, he had only two or three months to become familiar with his unique command, select and train a crew, and make all the myriad other preparations for the tour.

The chronology of the *Constitution's* commanding officers maintained by the USS Constitution Museum states that he was "remembered as an excellent public relations man, not a leader." [8] This seems to be selling him at least a little bit short. There is evidence in the record of some good leadership traits, including good communication skills, a sense of humor, willingness to praise and give credit to subordinates and to be a cheerleader for the command. One of the Marines in the crew, Corporal John Waller, regarded his old Captain well enough to send him a Christmas card every year. [9]

In any case, an excellent public relations man was exactly what was needed for this assignment, and judging by the results, Gulliver succeeded spectacularly. Occasionally, the Navy does manage to put the round peg in the round hole.

Twice during the tour, in Beaumont, Texas, and San Diego, California, Gulliver was ill enough that he had to be hospitalized for several days. The nature of the illness in San Diego was reported as "a severe cold." [10] It might well have been stress related. The National Tour of the *Constitution* was no pleasure cruise for the officers and

Letter and drawing of the USS *Constitution*
by Mary Gail Gulliver, from Commander
Gulliver's scrapbook.

men of the *Constitution* and its tender, the minesweeper USS *Grebe*. At sea, there was the strain of keeping a national treasure safe while under tow, an evolution requiring undivided attention and skillful seamanship in the best of circumstances. In port, there was the near daily grind of tours, demonstrations and public relations events ashore, maintaining a cheerful disposition while managing the large crowds of visitors, and keeping the inevitable souvenir hunters from picking the old ship clean. In San Pedro, California, one enterprising thief managed to get away with a 24 pound solid shot for the cannons.[11] They may not have been at sea for long periods of time, but except for occasional leave periods, they were away from their homes and families.

Most Navy fathers (and mothers, these days) with children of a literate age have received a letter, at one time or another, like this one to Commander Gulliver from his daughter Mary:

"Dearest Daddy,

We just received your telegram this morning and were very glad it came. When are you coming home? I am trying to be a very good girl while you have been away.

Very much love to my daddy,

Mary Gail Gulliver" [12]

Mary was eight years old at the time.

Commander Gulliver and an unidentified officer with the *Constitution's* Marines. (*Naval History and Heritage Command, photo NH58925*)

Chapter 3
Officers and Crew

THE CONSTITUTION SAILED on the National Tour with a normal complement of seven Officers, 65 enlisted Sailors and 15 enlisted Marines. The initial wardroom consisted of:

Commander Louis J. Gulliver, Commanding
Lieutenant Commander J. H. Carson,
   Executive Officer
Lieutenant C.A. Swofford, First Lieutenant
Lieutenant H. St. John Butler, Navigator
Lieutenant A.D Clark, Gunnery and Engineering
Lieutenant B.O. Kilroy (Supply Corps),
   Supply and Disbursing
Lieutenant H. D. Templeton (Medical Corps),
   Medical Officer.

In her heyday, Old Ironsides was home to more than 400 men, including about 50 Marines. [1]

⚓ BLUE JACKETS

No record has been found yet as to how Commander Gulliver selected the enlisted sailors for the tour or how they were organized into divisions and departments. He was no doubt looking for reliable men with clean records who would make a favorable impression on the public. A muster list with 83 names on it survives in a scrapbook compiled by a crew member, but does not include the members rank, rate and branch of service. It is divided into seven groups, indicating that there might have been seven divisions. [2]

The Enlisted Personnel Report was periodically included in the Deck Logs. It showed that the enlisted allowance was 60 Sailors and 15 Marines. Gulliver was usually between five and ten in excess on sailors and fully manned with Marines. The allowance by rate was as follows:

- Boatswain's Mate / Coxswain – 5
- Gunner's Mate – 1
- Quartermaster – 3
- Signalman – 1
- Seaman First Class – 16
- Seaman Second Class – 16
- Carpenter's Mate – 1
- Shipfitter – 2
- Sailmaker – 1
- Painter – 1
- Yeoman – 1
- Storekeeper – 2
- Pharmacist's Mate – 1
- Bugler – 1
- Commisaryman / Ship's Cooks – 3
- Officer's Stewards –1
- Mess Attendants – 4 [3]

The "Iron Men" of the tour, those who had been crew members for the whole duration of the tour, were identified in *Our Navy* magazine in October, 1934. Twenty-nine Sailors and two Marines were "Iron Men." [4]

The *Constitution* could also call on the ship's force of the *Grebe* for any problems she might not be able to handle on her own. No matter what rating badge was on their sleeve, everyone had to be a Tour Guide, First Class. Two pamphlets were prepared for all hands, one summarizing the physical characteristics and facts about the *Constitution* and the other about her history, both perhaps, authored by Commander Gulliver.

Whatever the selection criteria for the crew was, it turned out that they were not exactly choir boys. Reading through the *Constitution*'s deck logs, Gulliver was holding disciplinary Captain's Mast two or three times a month. The most common offenses, as always, were Absent Over Leave or Absent Without Leave, but other infractions included:

- Improper conduct in connection with visitors [!]
- Leaving post or station without being properly relieved
- Asleep on watch
- Creating a disturbance
- Incapacitated for duty (drunk)
- Improper performance or neglect of duty
- Obscenity, unmilitary conduct
- Disobedience, insolence
- Assault, striking another person in the Navy
- Out of uniform
- Breaking arrest

Four Marines and two Sailors deserted during the course of the tour. [5]

By way of comparison, the *Grebe*, with a slightly smaller crew, also held Captain's Mast about twice a month. The vast majority of offenses were late returning from liberty, from a few minutes to several days. Over the course of the National Tour, the *Grebe* had one deserter and awarded bad conduct or undesirable discharges to six others. A *Grebe* deck log entry for September 18, 1933, notes that a petty officer and a man receiving a bad conduct discharge

Constitution Boatswain's Mate at the Grog Tub.
(Naval History and Heritage Command, photo 2248)

were sent ashore to buy civilian clothes for the man being discharged. Apparently, part of a bad conduct discharge at that time was surrendering your uniform. [6]

⚓ LEATHERNECKS

A good picture of the Marine Corps contribution to the National Tour emerges from an article Commander Gulliver wrote for *Leatherneck* magazine in June of 1938. The article is an ode to the versatility, virtue and valor of the United States Marine, enough to bring tears to the eyes of the most hardened Gunnery Sergeant. Gulliver certainly knew how to write for his audience.

> "I had come to Washington direct from Panama and Nicaragua where I served afloat in the Old Rochester. Here at first hand, her Marines had shown what they were capable of doing on board ship; there was no ship duty, outside the engineer department, that her Marines had no efficient hand in. Numbering close to 200, under Captain Frank Whitehead, they functioned in the ship's galley and in her storerooms; they were orderlies, of course, and they manned some of the ship's power boats as coxswains, engineers and bow-hooks. At least one Marine was in the signal gang, others were in the fire control party and the gun crews of the secondary battery were exclusively Marines." [7]

The *Rochester*'s normal complement was 565, which probably included no more than 40 Marines. If an additional 160 were aboard, either the *Rochester* was very crowded, or some blue jackets had been put ashore and their duties taken up by the leathernecks. In any case, they greatly impressed the ship's Executive Officer. Gulliver wanted Marines in the *Constitution's* crew for historical

"Mickey" Moran, a *Constitution* sailor aloft,
San Diego, California, 1933. *Photo by Robert Hoffer.*
(USS Constitution Museum Collection, 1539.6.)

reasons; they had always been a vital part of her crew in the past, and because they were willing to try any new task that might be set before them the Marines would be valued for the tour.

The Marines on the *Constitution* acted as cabin orderlies, acting as a buffer between the crowds of visitors and the Captain and his quarters. Gulliver wrote: "Only the patience of a saint and the soul of a diplomat sufficed for the job of being cabin orderly in the *Constitution*." They provided muscle for the fire and bilge pump and the anchor windlass, stood gangway and fire watches and provided an honor guard for distinguished visitors. They lived where their forebears lived, in a compartment on the orlop deck with only four feet, two inches of headroom. When docking and undocking with civilian tug boats, the two Marine Corporals amidships acted as the eyes and ears of the Captain on the poop deck, relaying signals to and from the tugs and making sure the *Constitution*'s masts and rigging stayed clear of obstacles on the pier. [8]

The usual strength of the Marine detachment was one Sergeant, two Corporals and twelve Privates. Headquarters Marine Corps, recognizing the public relations value of the tour to the Corps as well as the Navy, made sure replacements to the detachment were provided as needed. In the small Marine Corps of the 1930s even routine duty station changes were of interest to its members and transfers to and from the frigate were reported in *Leatherneck* magazine.

USS *Grebe* (AM-43) in the Harbor of New York.
(Library of Congress photo)

Chapter 4

The USS *Grebe* —
Faithful Servant of Old Ironsides

THE USS *GREBE* was a Lapwing class Minesweeper, part of the great expansion of the mine force for the First World War, commissioned on May 1, 1919. She conducted routine duties with the Atlantic Fleet, was decommissioned for overhaul in May 1922, and re-commissioned in December 1922. In 1930, she carried a medical team and relief supplies to the Dominican Republic, after that nation was devastated by a hurricane. [1]

Returning to Boston in 1931, the *Grebe* took on her most notable and memorable assignment. She was selected to be the tender for the United States' frigate *Constitution*, the venerable Old Ironsides, for the ship's National Tour.

Secretary of the Navy Charles F. Adams, an experienced yachtsman, had made inquiries about conducting the National Tour under sail. He was soon dissuaded of this. Writing in the U.S. Naval Institute's *Proceedings*, the Secretary's son noted that Admiral C. F. Hughes had told the Secretary, "Mr. Secretary, if you want to man her adequately, you will have to decommission a squadron of destroyers. Beyond that, I don't know who we could get to take command and train the crew." Undaunted, Secretary Adams interviewed a couple surviving square rigger captains who made the same assessment — "Not on your life, Mr. Adams. Sailing a ship like the *Constitution* is a lost art." [2]

So it was that the *Grebe* was signed on for the National Tour. She would tow the frigate from port to port, provide electrical power and messing for the *Constitution*'s crew in port and provide radio communications services as well. The muscle for this endeavor was provided by two Babcock and Wilcox oil fired boilers and a single triple expansion reciprocating steam engine. This would push an unencumbered *Grebe* through the water at 14 knots or allow her to pull heavy mine sweeping gear, (or a 2,250 ton sailing ship), at a much lower speed. It was a simple propulsion plant, and well maintained by *Grebe's* Engineering Department, it provided exceptionally reliable service. Over the three years of the National Tour, there were only seven engineering casualties logged:

- The water glass on No. 1 boiler blew out twice (once while under repair)
- a hot thrust bearing
- loss of feed water and loss of condenser vacuum (on the same day)
- a valve stem broke in the main sea water circulation system, and
- a fuel oil contamination casualty.

All were cleared quickly and the plant made ready to answer all bells. [3]

Even with no canvas spread, the *Constitution* has considerable sail area. Again from Mr. Adams' *Proceedings* article: "Once in a strong head wind, the *Constitution's* bluff bow and big rig, even with sails furled, created so much windage that the *Grebe* found herself making sternway. Later, with a following wind and sea, the *Grebe* found herself being overtaken by the *Constitution*, sails still furled, clipping along at a snappy 14 knots! The *Grebe* had no choice but to cast off the towline, fall in astern, and try to keep up." [4]

That makes a great story, but the author failed to find any mention of such an incident in either the *Constitution* or *Grebe* deck logs. Could it be that Commander Gulliver was indulging Secretary Adams in a bit of a sea story? There is no doubt, however, that Old Ironsides caught a lot of wind. On March 22, 1933, while lying off San Francisco waiting for the fog to lift, the *Grebe* was making 114 rpm in the face of force 5 winds just to stay in position. [5]

The standard bell for towing the *Constitution* was making 118 rpm at 195 psi main steam pressure. At this throttle setting, the tow typically proceeded at between 7 and 8 knots. Speed over ground varied with wind and seas, of course, the highest noted in the *Constitution*'s night order book being 11 knots and the lowest 2 knots. The *Constitution*'s night order book regularly admonishes the Officer of the Deck to mind the strain on the tow cable, stating that the bight should be touching the water. In open water, the standard amount of tow cable out was 150 fathoms. [6] Communications with the *Grebe* (presumably by flashing light at night) were to be constantly maintained and a test signal sent every half hour. The night order entry for April 1, 1934, reads, "Keep careful watch on *Grebe* for changes in speed. In case she slows, shear out sharply to leeward and be prepared to slip the towing cable." It must have been fairly nerve wracking for both crews. [7]

Naturally, the *Grebe* was somewhat overshadowed by her famous charge. As reported by the *Orange Leader* (March 17, 1932), "Life aboard the *U.S. Minesweeper Grebe*, getting no more attention than the pianist when the prima donna sings, is not the beer and skittles it used to be." [8] Nevertheless, Commander Gulliver tried to make sure the officers and men of the *Grebe* were included in

"Rozina" and "Scrappy." *Franciezek "Frank" Prusz's National Cruise Scrapbook, 1931–1934, page 53. (USS Constitution Museum Collection, 1869.1)* [13]

all of the various banquets, balls and picnics that were held wherever Old Ironsides touched port. The *Grebe's* complement while assigned as tender to the *Constitution* was three or four officers and around 50 enlisted. The Wardroom included a Lieutenant in command, sometimes a Lieutenant Junior Grade as Executive Officer, a Warrant Bosun, and a Warrant Machinist. Senior enlisted often stood Officer of the Deck watch, both in port and underway. [9]

Popular with the press were the *Grebe's* two mascots, "Rozina," a rhesus monkey and "Shanghai," a mid-sized German Shepherd mix. Rosie had been stolen from the ship by a boy in New York, where she passed through the hands of several owners until one was only too glad to return her to the ship. Like some sailors, she could never behave herself ashore and was only happy at sea. She had to be confined in port, as she had an aversion to small boys and had even bitten one. In New Orleans, she managed to break out of the brig and went missing again. By departure time, Rosie had still not mustered back aboard, and with a heavy heart, the *Constitution* and the *Grebe* proceeded down the river. As they reached the mouth of the Mississippi, a seaplane approached, landed nearby, taxied over to the *Grebe* and delivered the simian sailor back to her delighted crew. Rosie tormented Shanghai on occasion, but mostly they got along, and Shanghai would mope and refuse his mess when Rosie was missing. [10]

While visiting Grays Harbor, Washington, in July 1933, the local Naval Reserve Unit gifted the *Grebe* with another four legged crew member, a four month old black bear cub named "Commodore Scrappy," or just "Scrappy" for short. What the commanding officer of the *Grebe*, Lieutenant Harry St. John Butler, thought of this gesture of Total Force

USS *Constitution* and USS *Grebe* at Smith's Cove, Washington.
(Library of Congress photo)

Solidarity is not recorded. Under the care and feeding of the *Grebe*, Scrappy put on weight fast. On October 12, 1933, the *Long Beach Free Press* headlined "Bear Pet on USS Grebe Crew's Biggest Problem." He was kept secured on the after deck at sea, where the crew, tough sailors that they must have been, would stop by to rough house with him. Shanghai and Rosie kept a respectful distance. [11] About a month later, the *San Diego Union* reported that Scrappy had reached 150 pounds and featured a photo of a *Grebe* sailor giving him his daily ration of one quart of ice cream. [12] When he was mustered out of the service was not recorded. One might speculate that inquiries were made to the famous San Diego Zoo. [13]

An unidentified newspaper clipping in Volume 3 of the *Constitution* scrapbooks (see notes on sources) is an artist's depiction of the commercial tug *MV Shaver* towing the *Constitution* up the Columbia River, indicating that commercial towing services were contracted for at least once. [14] For both the north bound and south bound legs between the Panama Canal and San Diego, the *Constitution* was towed by the old submarine tender USS *Bushnell* (AS-2). [15] The *Grebe* remained in company. Why this was done is not documented, but the *Bushnell*, being a somewhat larger and more powerful ship, typically made 10 knots with the *Constitution* in tow, which would have saved appreciable time on this long leg. Navy and commercial harbor tugs were frequently used to move the *Constitution* out to open water where the *Grebe* could attach the towing cable. Where such services were unnecessary or unavailable, the *Grebe* would typically tie up alongside the *Constitution* to convey her away from the pier and pass the towing cable over when they reached more open water. [16]

For the final leg of the tour, coming up the East Coast

USS *Bushnell* AS-2. *(Naval History and Heritage Command, photo NH 668)*

from Florida, the tug USS *Umpqua* (AT-25) was also in company, presumably as a back up to the *Grebe*. Perhaps having made it that far, the Navy was taking no more chances with the old ship. [17]

The *Constitution*'s National Tour was completed in May 1934. The *Grebe* received the following from Commander Gulliver of the *Constitution*:

Navy Yard Boston, Mass.
10, May, 1934

TO THE GREBE, HER CAPTAIN, OFFICERS AND CREW

I am sorry to have you go away from us forever. No ship could ever have such a fine, efficient, faithful and loyal friend. You never failed us — in calm or storm, in port or at sea. A wonderful ship, the GREBE, and a grand crew, officers and men. God bless you.

Louis J. Gulliver
Commander, USN, Commanding [18]

The *Grebe* continued to provide varied support to the Atlantic Fleet until June 1940, when she arrived at Pearl Harbor to provide similar services to the Pacific Fleet. She was at Pearl Harbor undergoing a yard availability on December 7, 1941, when the Japanese struck. Her 3-inch guns had been dismantled for the overhaul, but she was credited with shooting down a Japanese plane with small arms fire.

In June 1942, the *Grebe* was re-designated as a fleet tug (AT-134), as were several other Lapwing class minesweepers. She met her end on December 6, 1942, while unsuccessfully attempting to refloat a grounded cargo ship in the Fiji Islands. A hurricane destroyed both ships on the first and second of January 1943, before they could be salvaged. She was stricken from the Naval Register on July 28, 1943.[19]

LOOKING FORWARD

A crowd gathers to tour the ship in San Diego, 1933. Looking from bow of *USS Constitution* to the crowded dock below in San Diego, California, 1933. *Photo by Robert Hoffer.*
(USS Constitution Museum collection, 1539.4)

Chapter 5

The Tour

ON JULY 31, 1931, Mr. Howard Wood, a photographer in New Bedford, Massachusetts, watched the *Constitution* arrive for her visit to that port. A group of children were playing nearby. In a letter to Commander Gulliver dated May 11, 1932, Wood described the scene:

> " The children ceased their play and stood silent as *their* 'Constitution' with lofty masts towering in silhouette against a gorgeous sunset sky, swept grandly in to visit them." (emphasis in the original) [1]

It was a scene repeated in each of the 76 U.S. ports that the *Constitution* touched over the next three years. A full itinerary is provided in Appendix II. In general, the National Tour took part in two major segments. From July 1931, until May 1932, she made her way from Boston down the East Coast and Gulf Coast, returning to Washington D.C., to remain there until December 1932. Passing through the Panama Canal over the New Year of 1933, she arrived in San Diego, on January 21, 1933, and made her way up the West Coast as far north as Bellingham, Washington, in July and was back in San Diego in November. She wintered in San Diego until March 1934, passing through the canal again in April and made just a couple more stops before returning to Boston on May 7, 1934.

No other city was more interested in the progress of the National Tour than Boston, where Old Ironsides was built and home ported through most of her history. No other newspaper covered the tour more thoroughly than the *Boston Globe*. Many articles about the tour can be found in the *Globe's* archives.

The fair city of Boston was not immune to the ills of the time, however. A script for a radio broadcast announcing the ship's visit warned visitors to beware of pickpockets and leave valuables at home. [2] The tour would be troubled by thieves, con-men and hucksters at several ports of call.

The *Constitution* was in Portsmouth, New Hampshire, for the Fourth of July holiday, 1931. During her first six days there, she received 22,779 visitors, a fairly typical number. [3] Leaving Portsmouth, the ship's log reported "considerable difficulty raising anchor due to faulty operation of the messenger chain on the capstan." [4]

On July 15, 1931, she was at Bath, Maine, where the officers and men of the *Constitution* and the *Grebe* were presented with the Keys to the City. [5]

At Bar Harbor, Maine, more difficulties with the ground tackle were experienced and overcome. Commander Gulliver held a meritorious mast on July 23, 1931, to commend members of the seaman gang for anchor handling at Bar Harbor "under hazardous and trying conditions." [6]

Marblehead, Massachusetts, claiming to be the birth place of the United States Navy, was reached on July 29. A 21 gun salute was received from Fort Sewell. The *Globe* reported, "The school children have pooled their pennies and will present the old battleship with a beautiful silver vessel." [7] His Excellency Mr. A. C. Ratchetsky, Minister to Czechoslovakia, called on the Captain. [8]

In New Bedford, Massachusetts, on August 5, 1931, a visitor fell down the port ladder and was bruised, being attended to by the Medical Officer and the Pharmacist's Mate. This is the only instance of an injury to a visitor found in the deck logs over the whole duration of the cruise, perhaps the most remarkable achievement of the whole tour. [9]

In New York, the arriving *Constitution* was overflown by the massive German DO-X trans-Atlantic seaplane and nearly 100 other aircraft. [10] The temptations of the big city were too much for some of the crew. On the fifth day in port, five Marine Privates missed morning muster. Four never returned and were declared deserters after 10 days absence. The next evening, two Quartermasters went on a toot and were "brought on board under guard and under the influence of intoxicating liquor." Gulliver came down hard on the two. The more senior man was restricted for 30 days and lost $12 per month for 6 months. The junior man lost a stripe. [11]

The tour schedule was altered slightly so that the ship could be in Philadelphia for Constitution Day on September 17, 1931. The tour dates for Philadelphia and Wilmington, Delaware, were exchanged to accommodate the Philadelphia City Fathers. [12] In Philadelphia, there was the first really big crowd—25,743 visitors being logged on September 27. There was more trouble ashore. A Seaman First Class returned from liberty sober, but with a puncture wound to one cheek and was stitched up by Lieutenant Templeton. [13]

From October 16 to October 23 the *Constitution* was in Yorktown, Virginia, to celebrate the 150th Anniversary of Lord Cornwallis' surrender. Also present were the Battleships *Arkansas* and *Wyoming* and, representing France, the new cruisers *Suffren* and *Dusquene*. [14] French General D'Ollone and his aide visited the ship on the 17th, followed by Admiral Leahy, Secretary of the Navy Adams and the Assistant Secretary for War the next day. President

Hoover viewed the festivities from on board the battleship *Arkansas* on the 19th. The *Grebe* also manned the rail in honor of the President on October 19. [15]

In October 1931, the tour ran into severe head-winds in the form of the 1933 budget for the Navy Department. Not only was the tour to be ended early and Old Ironsides tied up, but the Boston Navy Yard was to be closed. The political firestorm that ensued from depression-hit Boston can be imagined. The Boston chapter of the Veterans of Foreign Wars fired off an angry missive to the Navy Department, which drew an equally testy response from Secretary Adams:

> "Dear Mr. Weldman, I would be very much obliged to my friends of the Veterans of Foreign Wars if they could indicate to me how to achieve the necessary savings of about $50,000 without closing the Boston Navy Yard and laying up Old Ironsides." [16]

Worse, there was talk of Old Ironsides not returning to Boston, but being maintained as a museum in either the Washington Navy Yard or at the Naval Academy. The redoubtable Congressman John W. McCormack fired a broadside at the Hoover administration, accusing it of keeping the *Constitution* down south only because it would make it easier to close the Boston Navy Yard. The cost of returning the ship to Boston in tow of a commercial tug was only $2,000, he pointed out, so surely funding was not the real reason. The pressure from the Massachusetts Congressional delegation and elsewhere on the Hoover administration was being felt by November 1931, when the President himself visited the ship, denting his felt hat on the low overheads and announcing that the Navy Department "may resume the abandoned southern cruise sometime next year." Less than a week later, the *Globe* reported that "Secretary Adams said today that 'The Navy

Department is glad to announce that funds have been released for the purpose of continuing the cruise.'" [17]

The *Constitution* was at Annapolis, where she had once been the school ship, from November 2 to November 5. Her draft was too deep to allow her to tie up along the Severn River sea wall, so she was anchored off Greenbury Point and visitors brought out by craft identified by the *Washington Post* as "sub chasers," possibly Naval Academy training craft — Yard Patrol (YP) boats. The *Post* also reported that Maryland Senator Millard Tydings was leading a fight to have the *Constitution* permanently based at Annapolis. During this visit, she was overflown by the giant Navy airships *Akron* and *Los Angeles*, based in Lakehurst, New Jersey. [18] Midshipmen toured the ship, helped organize the visitors and manned the capstan to weigh her anchor on departure. No doubt more than one struggling Mid was inspired to put just a little more effort into his training. The Superintendent, Rear Admiral Thomas C. Hart, visited the ship on November 5. [19] On November 10, the Washington Navy Yard installed two 1-pounder saluting guns and provided 100 rounds of ammunition. There was a lot of saluting to be done. That afternoon the President, Mrs. Hoover, Secretary Adams and the Chief of Naval Operations visited. On November 12, salutes were fired to the Commandant of the Marine Corps, General Fuller, and Vice Admiral Haggard, Royal Navy, Commander in Chief of the American and West Indies Squadron in port aboard the cruiser HMS *Dehli*. The saluting battery was returned to the Navy Yard on the 17th. [20]

The *Constitution* departed the Washington Navy Yard on November 18, 1931, for her tour of the Southern and Gulf Coast ports. The citizens of Brunswick, Georgia, and Pensacola, Florida, took a special interest in the ship in that live oak timbers for her original construction had

USS *Constitution* at Pensacola. *(Library of Congress photo)*

come from Brunswick and timbers for her most recent re-construction had been found in Pensacola.

The Pensacola City fathers took note of Commander Gulliver's gift for oratory in a thank-you letter back to him: "As you, Captain Gulliver, in speaking of her age to some of us remarked, 'Years do not count with her; she was called back into this holy commission by the poetic spirit of the nation, and by it she will ever be renewed.'" [21]

In Key West, a new officer reported aboard. Lieutenant J. W. Dannenberg was assigned general duties as a Watch and Division Officer. [22]

While the ship was at Jacksonville, Florida, a story surfaced about a man claiming to be the *Constitution*'s "publicity agent." He traveled about three weeks ahead of the tour, selling unauthorized pamphlets and causing other trouble. Gulliver asked the Justice Department to "stop this unauthorized practice which is resulting in much undesirable feeling towards the *Constitution*." [23]

Big crowds awaited in Houston, with 26,638 visitors being logged on February 26, 1932, and 31,005 on the February 28. [24]

Commander Gulliver was taken ill in Beaumont, Texas, and had to be hospitalized with a diagnosis of "myositis, acute" which covers a wide range of auto-immune inflammations.[25] Lieutenant Commander Carson took over to maintain the tour schedule. Carson would remain in charge for nearly a month. [26] By the time Tampa was reached in early April 1932, Gulliver was back in form. The Tampa customs office wrote to the Assistant Secretary of the Navy: "I want you to know that we were very appreciative to have the *U.S. Frigate Constitution* with us and that Commander Louis J. Gulliver added interest to the visit because of his charming personality." [27] That was just one of many similar accolades collected by Gulliver in his scrapbooks.

USS *Constitution* entering Corpus Christie, Texas, February 1932.
(Naval History and Heritage Command photo)

The *Constitution's* masts, at over 200 feet above the waterline, initially prevented her from going up the Houston ship channel from Galveston due to overhanging high tension wires, a problem that would be encountered with bridges and wires elsewhere on the tour. [28] In New Orleans, on January 27, 1932, the *Grebe's* deck log noted that the tow did not pass under the high tension lines until the power had been shut off. [29]

In the 1930s, there were still a few old salts around who had served on the *Constitution* when she was an apprentice training ship in the 1880s. Occasionally, one would show up for a teary-eyed tour, the most notable being one Charles Nowak, age 76 of Lewis Island (St. Petersburg), Florida. As reported in the *Boston Globe:*

" The first thing he did was express his happiness in weeping. Then he chased about the deck like a boy, inspecting everything with minute care. He was a bit disappointed at the changes made in the old frigate. He climbed up the rope ladder of the towering mizzen mast with the nimbleness of a cat and frolicked in the rigging to the great anxiety of the sightseers below. Finally, Commander F. J. [sic] Gulliver spied him and ordered him to come down. The command was heeded with much grumbling. Thereafter the old sailor contented himself with taking the breath of landlubbers by skipping along the bulwarks." [30]

The old man, who called himself "Gun Captain, Gun # 11," seemed to have happier memories of his time on board than the record would indicate. He was an apprentice, a Third Class Boy, who had been aboard for about five months in 1881, failing the exam for the next higher rank.[31]

From St. Petersburg, the *Constitution* and *Grebe* returned to the Washington Navy Yard in April 1932, where she would remain until the following December, conducting some routine repairs, rotating some crew members and hosting some notable visitors, including the British Ambassador, his wife and Mrs. C. F. Adams. Among the personnel detached was the Executive Officer, Lieutenant Commander Carson, on April 30. [32]

A tour for the sightless in the area was conducted on April 18, something that would also be done in some of the larger cities visited. [33]

The ship experienced the scare of the tour during a brief visit down the Potomac to Alexandria on May 12, 1932. As reported in the *Washington Post*, with more than 50 visitors aboard and the *Grebe* made up alongside, she started dragging her anchor in a high wind. Quick action on the part of Commander Gulliver and the *Grebe* brought the situation under control before any damage was done. [34] The ship's log recorded the incident as follows:

> 16:03 – commenced dragging anchor for about 300 yards, put starboard anchor on the cat head and cleared ship of visitors [presumably by boat or launch]
>
> 16:14 – Grebe shoved off from alongside
>
> 16:23 – took tow line from Grebe.
>
> 16:36 – commenced heaving in port anchor
>
> 17:10 – underway in tow of Grebe [35]

The *Grebe's* deck log reported this incident more matter-of-factly, with some variance in the times logged for the major events:

> 16:01 – Wind increasing, starting to drag anchors
>
> 16:10 – Cast off from Constitution
>
> 16:25 – passed tow line to Constitution
>
> 16:40 – Underway for Washington Navy Yard
>
> 18:20 – Arrived at Washington Navy Yard, cast off tow line [36]

She was quickly returned to her berth at the Washington Navy Yard and the visitors put ashore. Gulliver congratulated the crew for their quick response to the drag at muster on May 14. [37]

Among the crew replacements reporting aboard while the ship was in Washington was a new Executive Officer, Lieutenant Commander Henry Hartley. Hartley was a salvage expert, having participated in the salvage of the submarines S-4 and S-51 before his tour on the *Constitution*. He would also be the salvage officer for the submarine USS *Squalus* in 1939. He had been awarded the Navy Cross for his duty as Captain of the Submarine Rescue Ship USS *Falcon* during the salvage of S-4. [38]

Hartley's eight month old son, Henry Jr., was christened on board on June 26, 1932, only the second time such a ceremony was performed on board, the first being of Mary Eastman, daughter of the ship's commander in 1866. [39]

The French Ambassador was honored on board for Bastille Day on July 14, 1932. [40]

Lieutenant Clark was detached on June 20, 1932. Lieutenant Dannenberg assumed duties as Gunnery and Engineering Officer.

While the *Constitution* waited at the Washington Navy Yard, the *Grebe* sailed to the Charleston, South Carolina, Navy Yard for a much needed overhaul. Upon completion, she returned to the Norfolk Naval Base and provided various towing and transport services to the Fleet up and down the Chesapeake Bay until it was time to resume her duties as tender to the *Constitution* in December. [41]

Tour or no tour, the Great Depression ground on. In the summer of 1932, the "bonus marcher" camp was visible from the *Constitution's* fighting tops at her berth in the Washington Navy Yard. On June 10, 1932, the ship received from the USS *Cormorant* and the Washington

Henry Hartley, as Commander, USN.
(Photo courtesy of Militaria Forum)

Navy Yard two Lewis machine guns with six magazines (four loaded, two empty), forty .30 caliber rifles with bayonets and cartridge belts, 2,400 rounds of .30 caliber ammunition and 500 rounds of .45 caliber ammunition. Apparently there was a concern that the bonus marchers might try to take over the ship and / or the Navy Yard. On July 28, 1932, the camp was burned and the marchers dispersed by troops under the command of General Douglas MacArthur, a sad and ugly incident. The small arms and ammunition were returned to the Navy Yard on August 3, 1932. [42]

Another new officer had reported on August 2, 1932, Lieutenant J. R. McKinney, assigned as a Watch and Division Officer and the Educational Officer. [43]

On August 9, the most serious breach of discipline occurred. A Seaman First Class assaulted a Gunner's Mate First Class leaving several severe lacerations, which were treated by the Navy Yard Medical Officer. Justice was swift. Captain's Mast referred the case to a Summary Court Martial. The Summary Court imposed a fine $31 a month for six months and a bad conduct discharge. The convening authority remitted the bad conduct discharge based on good behavior for the next six months. [44] There must have been some extenuating circumstances.

In September, Lieutenant W. J. Dean (Supply Corps) relieved Lieutenant Kilroy as Supply and Disbursing Officer. On September 3, a Seaman First Class "while skylarking in the mess hall, slipped and fell against a mess table, lacerating his forehead." He received two stitches from Doc Templeton. Boys will be boys. More business for the Medical Officer was on September 7, when a Boatswain's Mate lacerated his arm on untrimmed wire. [45]

In November 1932, Lieutenant Swafford was detached and Lieutenant H. T. Wray reported as First Lieutenant. He

Aftermath of the burning of the bonus marchers' camp, Washington, D.C., July 1932. The *Constitution's* masts are faintly visible in the far background. *(Naval History and Heritage Command, photo NH122385)*

would be aboard only a month, detaching on December 6. On November 16, the British Ambassador, Sir Roland Lindsey, Mrs. Lindsey, Secretary Adams and Mrs. Adams visited the ship. The German Ambassador, F. W. Von Prittwitz, visited on December 5. [46]

On December 8, 1932, the *Constitution* and the *Grebe* shoved off for the West Coast, stopping for a few days at the Guantanamo Bay Naval Base before proceeding to Cristobal, the Caribbean terminus of the Panama Canal. While at Guantanamo, a Marine private was sentenced to three days solitary on bread and water for insolence to the Chief Master at Arms. He was released from solitary the next day. On January 1, 1933, a Quartermaster Second Class was placed under guard. The reason was not given. He was probably drunk, and was restored to duty the next day. This seemed to be a pattern with Gulliver, he would impose a severe punishment and walk it back the next day. This was especially true in port, when it wouldn't do to have the brig occupied with visitors aboard. [47]

Note that in the photo on the following page, the *Grebe* is made up alongside the *Constitution*, the preferred arrangement for providing the tow in restricted waters. Balboa, the Pacific terminus, was reached on December 27, 1932, and left on January 7, 1933. While in Balboa, the ship was visited by the President of the Republic of Panama and the "envoy extraordinary and Minister Plenipotentiary of the USA to the Republic of Panama." The ship was dry-docked for two days for a bottom cleaning. On January 8, 1933, for the first time in 93 years, Old Ironsides' bottom touched the Pacific under tow of the *Grebe*. [48]

Towing duties for the long haul to San Diego were taken over by the USS *Bushnell* (AS-2) on January 13, with the *Grebe* in company. The *Grebe* was glad to have the help. The day before, she noted in her log increasingly strong

The *Constitution* and the *Grebe* in the Panama Canal —
East to West crossing. *(Library of Congress photo)*

winds and heavy seas, and shortened the towing cable by 50 fathoms.[49] Heavy weather was also encountered off the Gulf of Tehuantepec, testing the sturdiness of the restoration effort and opening some deck seams. San Diego was made safely on January 21. [50] As might be expected, a tumultuous welcome awaited her in that Navy town, including a flyover by some Navy flying boats and a salute from the USS *Raleigh*, flagship of Rear Admiral Leahy, Commander, Destroyer Force. [51]

A sail handling demonstration was held for some local dignitaries, including Sr. P.O. Rubio, former president of Mexico; Rear Admiral Thomas Senn, Commandant of the 11th Naval District; Mayor Forward; the British and Chilean counsels; and the head of the Chamber of Commerce. Fraud reared its ugly head again, with the citizens of San Diego being warned against unlicensed peddlers selling Constitution trinkets and, worse yet, tickets to get aboard! [52]

In San Diego, Gulliver out-sourced his brig problem, transferring a recalcitrant Marine Private to the facilities on the USS *Rigel* (AR-11) for five days confinement on bread and water. There were more changes in the Wardroom with Lieutenant B. E. Carter being detached and Lieutenant (junior grade) D. W. Tolson coming aboard as aide to the Commanding Officer, Watch and Division Officer. [53]

Another tour for the sightless was given in San Diego. On another day Chief Quartermaster Stowe, upon learning that an injured boy was waiting alone in the family car while his siblings toured the ship, dispatched Seaman Duponti and Seaman Schmid to carry the child aboard. Gulliver received a heartfelt thank you letter from the boy's mother, Mrs. John C. McCutcheon, a Navy wife. He routed it to the officers with the notation "It is a great pride, but not a surprise to get such a letter." [54]

Looking down onto *USS Constitution*, visitors can be seen crowding the spar deck, San Diego, California, 1933.

Photo by Robert Hoffer. (USS Constitution Museum collection, 1539.5)

In San Diego, Gulliver had to be hospitalized again, the illness reported in the media as "a severe cold," and Hartley took over. It was an unfortunate time for the Captain to be on the binnacle list. It was soon evident that enthusiasm for Old Ironsides was not limited to the East Coast. School children from as far away as Phoenix, Arizona, showed up to visit the ship in San Diego. [55]

It was in the Los Angeles area—San Pedro and Long Beach—that visitation records tumbled day after day.

The all-time daily visitor record was set at San Pedro on March 5, 1933, at 36,400! [56] Two other days exceeding 30,000 visitors were logged in San Pedro and several in excess of 20,000. The City of Los Angeles passed an ordinance to keep hucksters selling "official" souvenirs at least 1,000 yards away from the ship. The 1,000 yard limit was based on the fact that the line to visit the ship was often a quarter mile or more long in other ports visited. [57] In San Pedro, the line was said to have reached ten across and three miles long! [58]

A small boost to the local economy was noted by the *San Pedro News Pilot*. Ten extra men would be taken on by the H-10 water taxi company to shuttle visitors to the ship. [59]

Civic support to get visitors aboard, especially school children, was very strong. Los Angeles school children were granted half days off in rotations to visit the ship. Special trains were provided by Pacific Electric and the Southern Pacific Rail Road to bring children into San Pedro to visit the ship from communities such as Bakersfield, Santa Barbara and Santa Monica. The *Los Angeles Times* repeated a series of pleas for every citizen with an automobile to load up with kids and bring them to see the ship.[60]

Welcome as all this adulation was, Hartley and his crew started to be overwhelmed. Some of the only bad press the *Constitution* got was from the *San Pedro News Pilot*, noting with dismay that the visit was going to be cut short by two days due to "naval orders" and children would be left out. On March 1, 1933, Hartley established a priority system that moved school tour groups to the front of the line and extended visiting hours by 30 minutes from 10 AM to 5:30 PM. School groups from more distant communities were also moved ahead. "We would rather have children aboard than adults, because it is in the minds of the younger generation that we must instill the same patriotism that inspired the men of 'Old Ironsides' to the heroic deeds that more than a century ago saved the nation for us today," [61] Hartley said. The mayor, chief of police, port manager and other officials met with Hartley to explore various ways to solve the problem. Gulliver was due back from his sick leave the next day and surely Hartley was glad to see him. Hartley was no doubt thinking back fondly to days past on easier assignments, like salvaging sunken submarines in foul weather. On March 7, 1933, Gulliver announced that the visit would be extended by two days. Instead of taking two days for cleaning, painting and upkeep, those tasks would be performed during non-visiting hours. That probably went over better with the public than it did with the crew. In compensation, there was a dance in their honor scheduled ashore. (If they weren't still painting.) [62]

On March 10, 1933, the move over to Long Beach was made. That same evening, about supper time, the city was hit by a devastating earthquake, causing 120 fatalities and doing $50 million in damages (1933 dollars). [63] Gulliver described how it felt aboard the *Constitution*: "Other than a severe shaking, there was no damage done Old Ironsides during the recent earthquake. The ship trembled very violently and very heavily. This was accompanied by a blood-curdling roar, all of which made it seem certain that the ship was being completely destroyed. I did not know that it was an earthquake, and, therefore was completely dazed by the terrible feeling that this ship, to which I had given nearly two years to guarding and protecting her, was being destroyed, and we were helpless to save her." [64] The *Grebe* was also undamaged by the event. [65]

On March 15, in Long Beach, the ship was visited by the Commander in Chief of the US Fleet, Admiral Sellers, and a bevy of other brass hats. [66] On March 19, happy to leave the mobs and natural disasters of Los Angeles behind, the *Constitution* and the *Grebe* shoved off for Santa Barbara and the San Francisco Bay area. In addition to announcing and covering the ship's visits, newspapers took the opportunity to use stories about the ship's history and equipment as filler. "Girl Reporter" stories were popular at the time, one being reporter Anna Somer of the *San Francisco News* trying her hand at swabbing decks, tying knots, taking compass bearings and other nautical chores aboard Old Ironsides. [67]

On March 29, in San Francisco, Miss Gene Adelstein was recorded as being the three-millionth visitor to the ship. While the ship was at Oakland on April 14, 1933, the *Constitution* was visited by Vice Admiral Gengo Hyakutake, Imperial Japanese Navy, Commander of the Japanese Navy Training Squadron. The Admiral was accompanied by his staff and 150 Japanese Midshipmen. Some of these young men and their hosts would be facing each other under less friendly circumstances in just a few years. [68]

On April 6, a rumor of a bomb plot to damage the ship reached the Navy Intelligence Office. The ship was closed to visitors and searched with the assistance of the San Francisco Police Department and nothing was found. [69] The *Grebe* was also searched, with no evidence of "nefarious devices" being found. Three days later, however, the *Grebe's* in port watch accosted a man in naval uniform identifying himself as "Nick Clark Sharp." Suspected to be an imposter, he was escorted over to the *Constitution* under guard. What happened to him after that was not recorded. Most likely he was just a common thief, but he might have had more sinister motives. [70]

May found the *Constitution* and the *Grebe* in Astoria, Oregon, along with the French training cruiser RFS *Jeanne D'Arc*. [71] There was another rare instance of bad press in Astoria. One Mr. M. R. Chessman, editor of the *Astorian Budget*, had published a special "souvenir edition" of his paper and sent his salesmen to sell it to the crowds waiting in line to visit the ship. The hucksters were closer to the ship than Gulliver allowed for such activities and he had them chased off. Chessman later wrote an editorial and sent an open letter to the Navy Department decrying Gulliver's tyranny. The competition over at the *Astoria Daily Messenger* was quick to leap to Gulliver's defense: "Any pinhead would know that a blast from Chessman, or anyone else of his caliber, would draw no water with the Navy Department of the United States . . . " [72] Take that, Chessman! They just don't write 'em like that anymore.

Five Marine privates disgraced the Corps on the last night in Astoria, returning aboard drunk, disrespectful and profane. Gulliver had the lot of them transferred ashore under guard on May 25, while at Gray's Harbor/ Aberdeen, Washington. To what facility or command was not recorded. [73]

There were more Wardroom changes in late May and early June. Lieutenant J.W. Van Cleve and a new Medical Officer, Lieutenant D.W. Lyon (Medical Corps) reported aboard. Lieutenants McKinney, Butler and Templeton were detached. Lieutenant Butler didn't go very far, stepping across the pier to take command of the *Grebe*. Lieutenant Dannenberg took over from Butler as Navigator on the *Constitution*. [74]

The *Constitution* would spend most of June and July of 1933 in the Puget Sound, reaching Bellingham, Washington, the farthest point north for the west coast portion of the tour on July 15. The ship was in Anacortes, Washington, arguably the smallest port visited, from July 20 to July 26. When the ship was being moored in Anacortes, a sailor threw a heaving line with a lead weight attached to line handlers ashore. The weight caught young Donald Hume above the right eye, "which for him subtracted somewhat from the excitement of the landing." The incident would leave a scar that would last a lifetime. Hume would go on to row as a member of the winning 1936 Olympic crew team, as told in D. J. Brown's best seller, *The Boys in the Boat*. [75] As reported in the *Anacortes American*, 27,689 visitors toured the ship and the ship's post office stamped 11,305 letters and postcards while the ship was in Anacortes. In cooperation with the local Elks Lodge, a tour was arranged for 49 physically handicapped residents and 23 shut-ins. Commander Gulliver extended the ship's stay there by one day to accommodate residents from the outlying San Juan Islands. [76] The ship's arrival in Bellingham was reported locally as follows:

> "When the U.S. Frigate *Constitution* arrived in Bellingham from Everett about 3:30 PM in tow of the U.S. Minesweeper *Grebe* she was greeted not only by a roar of factory whistles and by thousands of persons who lined the waterfront, but also by a large crowd at the municipal pier where the famous 'sea eagle' will be moored until next Thursday." [77]

While not the hordes of San Pedro, the crowds in the Puget Sound ports were large. An interesting discrepancy occurs in the *Constitution*'s deck logs during this time. On June 26, 1933, while at Olympia, Washington, Miss Pauline Newman was logged as the four-millionth visitor. That would have required about 11,000 visitors a day, every day, since the three-millionth visitor was logged on March 29. On July 19, at Bellingham, Washington, Miss Inez Littlefield is also honored as the four-millionth visitor. Did somebody find a book-keeping error after Miss Newman was named? It may be only a coincidence that all the landmark visitors identified in the logs are unmarried women. Maybe the crew kept an eye out for a nice looking young lady to be so honored when the count got close enough. [78]

The Fourth of July holiday was celebrated at Bremerton, Washington. Nine men from the *Constitution* were sent to the Bremerton Naval Hospital for treatment of acute gastroenteritis. Perhaps some potato salad sat out for too long at a Fourth of July picnic ashore. [79]

The tour left the Puget Sound on July 30, revisited Astoria for two days and tied up at Portland, Oregon, on August 2, 1933. On July 31, a Captain's Mast was held for a Marine Private charged with disobedience and a Coxswain charged with drunkenness. The Sailor was awarded 10 days restriction and lowered quarterly marks. On August 7, the man did not make muster and was charged in absentia with AWOL while on restriction. On August 11, his body was discovered floating alongside the *Grebe*, the only fatality experienced during the tour. A board of inquest was convened under Lieutenant Van Cleve, but the findings were not found in the log. [80]

The tour crossed the Columbia River bar and headed back down the coast at the end of August, revisiting some major ports, including another two weeks in San Pedro and some smaller ports by-passed on the north bound leg.

Admiral Sellers came aboard again while the ship was in San Pedro. [81]

On November 3, 1933, the ship was back in San Diego where she would winter over until March of the next year. The *Los Angeles Times* reported that the frigate would winter in San Diego and that more than 4.5 million visitors had been hosted without any injuries (neglecting the one bruised shin in New Bedford and Donald Hume's scar). [82]

It was time to rest, re-organize and re-fit. Lieutenant Dannenberg was detached and Lieutenant Van Cleve took over as Navigator, Engineer, Communications Officer and Officer in Charge of the Marine Detachment, the first time that last billet appears in the logs. Apparently Gulliver thought that the Marines needed some commissioned officer supervision. Lieutenant W. F. Royal reported aboard as First Lieutenant and Lieutenant Commander Hartley took a well deserved six weeks of leave. On December 20, 1933, Lieutenant (Junior Grade) Tolson and Miss Helen Lee Turner were united in marriage aboard the ship. Another wedding aboard followed on March 17, 1934, when Commander Gulliver's daughter Grace was wed to Lieutenant (Junior Grade) Wells Thompson. [83]

Naturally, Miss Gulliver's nuptials got more coverage than Miss Turner's, being reported in *The Boston Globe* and by the *Portland Press* (Maine), at the very least. As described in the *Portland Press*: "Before a flower-decked altar in the captain's cabin of the historical old frigate *Constitution*, Miss Grace Whiting Gulliver, a summer resident of Falmouth's Foreside, became the bride of Lieutenant Wells Thompson, USN Saturday at San Diego." Lieutenant Thompson was serving aboard the San Diego-based destroyer USS *Barney* at the time. [84]

Gulliver's family followed the ship through much of the West Coast portion of the tour and Mrs. Gulliver attended various social and charitable functions in the ports visited. A headline from the *Long Beach Press Telegram* implied that they traveled on board, although this seems unlikely. Daughters Mary and Anne were quoted as saying:

> "'It's such fun on the ship,' they giggled. 'We know all the best places to play hide and seek. We know where the pantry is, too.'" [85]

It's possible that Gulliver let the children sleep on board in port on occasion. Gulliver's son also spent some of his summer leave from the Naval Academy on board.

The USS *Constitution* float in the 1934 Tournament of Roses parade won third place. Riding on the float were Mrs. Gulliver and the two younger daughters. [86]

On March 20, 1934, the *Constitution* left San Diego under the tow of the *Bushnell*, with one man AWOL. Tow was shifted back to the *Grebe* on March 29 and two days later, the *Grebe* had to slow to 85 rpm to clear a fuel oil contamination casualty. By the end of March, the AWOL man had not turned himself in or been apprehended, so he was declared a deserter and the paymaster sold off whatever personal effects he had left behind, in accordance with the regulations of the time. [87]

On the first of April, the *Grebe* unexpectedly slowed to one-third speed and the *Constitution* sheared out to starboard to avoid running up on her. [88] Unusually, the *Grebe* was having some trouble with her engineering plant that day, a loss of feed-water casualty and a loss of condenser vacuum casualty both being logged, which necessitated the reduced speed. [89] Gulliver cautioned the Officers of the Deck, in the night orders that evening: "Keep careful watch on Grebe for changes in speed. In case she slows, shear out sharply to leeward and be prepared to slip the towing cable to avoid collision." [90]

Balboa was reached in the morning and five days were spent there making some minor repairs. Divers from the USS *Mallard* provided support by conducting some repairs on the copper sheathing below the water line. Cristobal was reached on April 7, 1934, and the ship departed for St. Petersburg, Florida, the next day. While anchored at St. Petersburg, a squall with gale force winds arose about midday on the 18th and the second (starboard) anchor was let go as a precaution. [91]

The only other port visited before returning to Boston was Charleston, South Carolina. The new Spanish sail training ship *Juan Sebastian Del Elcano* was also in port there and the ships exchanged visits. Commander Gulliver was much impressed by the new steel hulled barquentine and her crew of Spanish Naval Cadets, who were proving that given experienced officers, young men new to the sea could sail a large sailing ship efficiently. Now that keeping to a tight schedule was no longer a factor, the itch to sail Old Ironsides under her own canvas arose again. "We're not going to let the Spaniards put anything over on us, " Gulliver was quoted as saying in *The Boston Globe*, the article also noting the high praise Gulliver had expressed for the *Elcano*'s handling. [92] (The *Elcano* is still sailing today, with her crew of cadets.) Whether Gulliver thought better of it or the plan was nixed higher up, the *Constitution* returned to Boston in tow of the *Grebe*, with the Naval tug *USS Umpqua* in company for good measure. Boston was reached on May 7, 1934, where she has remained ever since. The city welcomed her back with open arms. There were speeches, parades, awards, balls and all sorts of celebration. Her commissioning pennant was hauled down on June 8, 1934, and this chapter of her history was closed.

The deck and the port side gun battery. *USS Constitution*'s spar deck during the National Cruise, c. 1931–1934.

Photo by MGM Motion Picture Corp. (USS Constitution Museum collection, 1508.12)

Chapter 6

Tour Routines

⚓ AT SEA

EVEN THOUGH the *Constitution* was under tow at sea, her Captain and crew were still responsible for her safe navigation. Commander Gulliver's Night Order Book has the usual entries concerning courses to be steered, expected times and bearings to sight navigation aids and the ubiquitous "Call me if anything unusual occurs." [Other common instructions are to be mindful of the strain on the tow cable (the bight should be in the water) and to test communications with the *Grebe* every half hour. Presumably communications with the *Grebe* at night were by means of flashing light.]

As might be expected on a wooden ship, fire was a hazard to be feared. The night orders of April 9, 1932, include "no smoking on the spar deck after sundown and until sunrise." Four days later, the prohibition on smoking during the night was extended to all decks. Another fire hazard was the wood-fired galley stove that fed the *Constitution's* crew at sea. From the January 19, 1933, night orders: "Have a careful watch kept on galley fires until they are extinguished for the night. Charley Noble to be watched when lighting off and after lighting off in the morning." ["Charley Noble" denotes the galley smoke stack in contemporary in Naval parlance.]

USS *Constitution* sailors aloft, furling the mainsail, 1931.
(Naval History and Heritage Command photo)

On March 21, 1933:

"Have half hourly reports made as to safety of galley *fires (one cook* constantly on watch).*"

The usual four hour watch routine was kept at sea. [1]

⚓ IN PORT

The work day in port began at 8 AM. Most days, the ship was open to visitors starting at 10 AM, and continuing until 5 PM, Sundays included. The count of visitors for the day was kept by the Marine gangway watch using a mechanical clicker-counter such as coal fired ships used to count sacks of coal when coaling ship. [2] The total number of visitors for the day was noted in the deck log at the end of the 4–8 PM watch. Often, some small number of visitors is noted during the 8 PM – midnight watch, indicating that perhaps the crew was allowed to bring small parties of friends and relatives aboard after 8 PM. [3]

Sail handling and gunnery demonstrations were favorite events with the visitors. *The Washington Post* describes one held at the Washington Navy Yard in July of 1932:

> "While a bos'n's whistle piped a shrill discord, a swarm of twentieth century sailors unfurled and lanyarded into place the mizzen mast canvas of the USS *Constitution* at her mooring at the Washington Navy Yard. . . . . The modern seamen — some of them lads of but a year's service in the Navy — can man the nautical artillery of yore, too. To the clipped commands of a smartly uniformed lieutenant, a bare-torsoed gun crew demonstrated how the 32-pounder carronades were fired in the days of close locked sea fights. The gun crew, sweating but enjoying the ceremony, wore cutlasses at their

A *Constitution* gun crew, with cutlasses (and shirts).
James William Tytler's National Cruise Scrapbook, 1931–1934, page 68.
(USS Constitution Museum Collection, Tytler scrapbook photo)

hips and knives in their belts. They were ready to 'board the enemy' if the carronades didn't suffice for victory." [4]

In addition to the ship tours, a lot of public relations work went on ashore. Gulliver, his officers and occasionally senior enlisted sailors often gave lectures on various topics related to the ship to civic organizations and schools. Gulliver also made extensive use of the new media of radio, broadcasting interviews about the ship and tour from the local radio stations.

What better way to spread a little cheer than a quartet of lusty tars singing sea chanties? *Constitution* sailors provided this entertainment to many a Lions Club, Kiwanis and Rotary luncheon. The singers were identified by *Our Navy* as Seaman First Class E.D. Indigaro; Painter Third Class J. Dauphinias; Seaman First Class E.D. Morin; and Coxs'n N. Duponti. [5] This lineup apparently changed as necessary and was also supported by the Leathernecks on occasion. [6]

Days in port when the ship was closed to visitors were spent in cleaning up and minor repairs, and also to provide some rest and liberty for the crew.

Postal cachet mailed by Harry Moore aboard *USS Constitution* in Balboa, Panama Canal Zone, January 1, 1933.
(USS Constitution Museum Collection, 1484.6.)

Postal cachet mailed by Harry Moore aboard USS *Constitution* in Charleston, South Carolina, May 8, 1934. This is a letter sent to his sister, Mrs. A.E. Steinberger.
(USS Constitution Museum collection, 1484.5)

Chapter 7

The Naval Postmark Collectors

AS THE POSTAL SERVICE modernized around the turn of the twentieth century, mail services for naval personnel improved as well. The first Navy Post offices were established on August 15, 1908, aboard the USS *Illinois* (BB-7), USS Rhode Island (BB-17) and the USS Prairie (AD-5). A sailor who took an oath to properly safeguard the mails and received some rudimentary training in running a post office could be designated "Navy Mail Clerk" or "Assistant Navy Mail Clerk." Any rating could apply, but the mail clerks primarily came from the administrative ratings like Yeomen and Storekeepers. [1]

The shipboard post offices, like all post offices, made their ink stamps to cancel the stamps on the cards and letters mailed aboard that ship. Some were quite creative. As letters from "the far China Station" and other exotic locales made their way home, a new type of hobbyist arose, the Naval Postmark Collector. These enthusiasts were largely sailors, former sailors, and philatelists. They added to their collections by sending a "cover" to a ship of interest, a cover being a stamped and self-addressed envelope or post card. The Navy Mail Clerk would cancel the cover with his ship's ink stamp and mail it back to the collector. The hobby became popular enough that the Universal Ship Cancellation Society was formed in

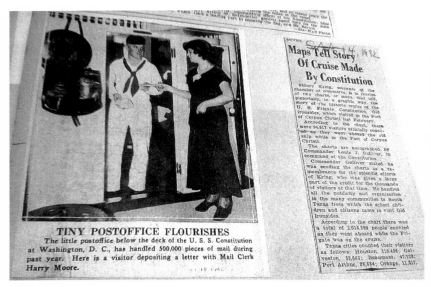

TINY POSTOFFICE FLOURISHES
The little postoffice below the deck of the U. S. S. Constitution at Washington, D. C., has handled 500,000 pieces of mail during past year. Here is a visitor depositing a letter with Mail Clerk Harry Moore.

Maps Tell Story Of Cruise Made By Constitution

Sidney Kring, manager of the chamber of commerce, is in receipt of two charts, or maps, that tell pictorially, in a graphic way, the story of the historic cruise of the U. S. Frigate Constitution, Old Ironsides, which visited in the Port of Corpus Christi last February.

According to the chart, there were 94,917 visitors officially counted—as they went aboard the old ship while in the Port of Corpus Christi.

The charts are autographed by Commander Louis J. Gulliver, in command of the Constitution.

Commander Gulliver stated he was sending the charts as a remembrance for the splendid efforts of Kring, who was given a large part of the credit for the thousands of visitors at that time. He handled all the publicity and organization in the many communities in South Texas from which the school children and citizens came to visit Old Ironsides.

According to the chart there was a total of 2,016,299 people counted as they went aboard while the Frigate was on the cruise.

Texas cities counted their visitors as follows: Houston, 118,496; Galveston, 32,663; Beaumont, 47,123; Port Arthur, 28,884; Orange, 11,517.

Storekeeper First Class Harry Moore and a visitor to his post office
(USS *Constitution National Tour Scrapbooks, U. S. Naval Academy, Nimitz Library*)

November 1932, with 15 members. [2] It's still in existence, with a current membership of about 1,400. [3]

A naval postmark has two parts, the cancel, which is the circle enclosing the ship's name and date and the "killer bars" or the lines that are stamped across the postage stamp so it can't be used again. Often mail clerks could add a unique message in between the killer bars.

On the previous page is an example of a cover the *Constitution*'s Mail Clerk, Storekeeper First Class Harry Moore, mailed back to himself at his Massachusetts home address. Notice the location (Balboa, Canal Zone) inserted in between the killer bars. The Canal Zone stamp adds to the uniqueness of this cover.

Naturally, no postmark became more coveted than one from Old Ironsides as she toured the country. Collectors large and small, serious and casual, and curious members of the public at large flooded the tiny post office (formerly the warrant officer's pantry) on the ship with covers.

Moore and his post office were a great public relations asset, as recognized by Commander Gulliver in an article for *Our Navy*:

> "I will give Our Navy readers of an outline of the perfectly gigantic task that Moore has carried out so cheerfully, tactfully and patiently for the half million that have all but overwhelmed him at times during the Cruise of the Constitution. . . . Through his unfailing courtesy, sympathy and patience with these cover collectors, Harry Moore has made thousands of friends for the Navy and *no* critics." (Emphasis in the original) [4]

A clipping from the *Portland Morning Oregonian* claimed that 36,000 covers had been canceled in one day while the ship was at San Pedro. [5] This seems somewhat

Petty Officer Moore, "with his canceling device gripped in his sturdy right arm." (USS *Constitution National Cruise Scrapbooks, U. S. Naval Academy, Nimitz Library*)

unlikely, as that would be one a second for 10 hours, but no doubt the volume was huge and sometimes Moore had help.

Newspaper clippings show that the public was encouraged to get their covers to the *Constitution* for stamping.

While the ship was at Long View, Washington, a special cover was sent to the sailor in the White House, Franklin D. Roosevelt. [6]

When the volume of mail and its importance to morale increased dramatically during World War II, the Navy established a separate Postal Clerk (PC) rating. This rating lasted until 2009, when the Postal Clerk and Storekeeper ratings were merged into the distinctly un-nautical sounding "Logistics Specialist" rating. [7]

The newly restored USS *Constitution* leaving Boston Harbor for the National Cruise, July 1931. *Photo by Leslie Jones.*
(USS *Constitution Museum collection, 2269.22*)

Epilogue

Thirty-four months on tour, 76 American cities visited, and more than 4 million visitors were received. The youngest visitor was not recorded. There were no doubt many a babe in arms brought aboard. The *Port Angeles News* reported the crew was particularly taken by three-year-old Miss Mary Louise Hinsmann, autographing her copy of *The Story of Old Ironsides* and plying her with ice cream. [1] The oldest visitor was Mrs. Maria C. Ryder of Avalon, California, at 93 years. As a young girl on the coast of Maine, she had watched Old Ironsides sail by. [2] Too frail to climb the gangway from a boat alongside, she was carried aboard by a Marine Corporal. Otherwise alert and curious, she told Commander Gulliver that "she didn't care when her hour came — she had seen and been on board the *Constitution.*" [3] It was surely a memorable experience for all but the most jaded visitors, as a visit to Old Ironsides still is today. Navy veterans, in particular, feel something special when walking the decks where so much of our naval tradition was formed. Visitors who might have come aboard for only something to do on a Sunday afternoon left with a renewed sense of patriotism and appreciation for our early naval history. In tough times, it was a reminder that we had fought through adversity before and prevailed.

The Navy brass followed the tour closely and had been quite pleased with the result. Gulliver received a personal letter from Admiral Sellers, Commander in Chief U.S. Fleet, dated September 23, 1933:

> "The cruise of the *Constitution* under your command has been a memorable one and, as far as I know, unique in Naval History. The *Constitution* is a wonderful old ship and from all reports that I have heard, you and the officers and men under your command have done a good job." [4]

For Commander Gulliver, who had put so much effort into the cruise, such accolades were not enough. When the Navy selection board for promotion to Captain next met, Gulliver was not on the list of those to be wearing four stripes on their sleeves. He was officially notified of his retirement on March 14, 1935, with an effective date of June 30, 1935. It was a heavy, heavy blow. Possibly the most poignant item in the scrapbooks Gulliver kept is a letter of commiseration from a friend and Annapolis classmate, William T. Mallison, skipper of the USS *Oglala* at the time. It's a wonderful expression of friendship and sympathy.

Needless to say, the selection board's decision was also quite controversial. There wouldn't be as much public interest in a selection board decision until a couple decades later, when an obscure Engineering Duty Captain named Hyman G. Rickover was denied promotion to Rear Admiral. People within the Navy and without lobbied on Gulliver's behalf. Mr. R. M. Kaufman, editor of the *Washington Evening Star*, wrote to Admiral J. K. Taussig, urging the Navy to re-consider. The New Bedford Port Society sent a resolution to Congress asking for Gulliver's promotion. So did the San Diego Chamber of Commerce. It was not enough. The ghost of the *Orion* loomed in the background. In a personal letter to Gulliver dated November 6, 1934, Rear Admiral Richard Leigh, presumably a member of the selection board wrote: "The unfortunate experience with your collier command weighs — or did — much in the opinion of some members of the board." [5]

Gulliver continued to write for various publications in retirement, especially, *Shipmate*, the magazine of the Naval Academy Alumni Association. He died at Bethesda Naval Hospital on April 17, 1962, of carcinoma of the bladder. [6]

Louis J. Gulliver, his officers and crew, and probably all but a handful of the four-million visitors who came aboard during the National Tour are gone now. The ship remains in Boston, the place of her birth, well cared for by her current Commanding Officer and a crew of dedicated young men and women. Go see her if you can. It is unlikely that she will ever come to see you again.

USS *Constitution* Today

In Boston Harbor

The mission is still public relations.

Boarding Pike Drill

Gunnery Demonstration

Change of command, August 2015

Admiral Michelle Howard on the gun deck

All photos courtesy of the U.S. Navy

Appendix I

History and Technical Characteristics of the USS Grebe

USS *Grebe*	Lapwing Class Minesweeper
Laid down	25 May 1918
by the Staten Island Steamboat Company	
Launched	17 December 1918
Commissioned	1 May 1919
De-commissioned	12 May 1922
Re-commissioned	15 November 1922
Struck from the Naval Register	28 July 1943

Displacement	950 tons
Length overall	187 feet, 10 inches
Beam	35 feet, 6 inches
Draft	8 feet, 10 inches
Speed	14 knots
Complement (as minesweeper)	78
Armament	two three-inch, dual-purpose guns [1]

Appendix II

Itinerary, USS *Constitution* National Tour 1 July 1931 to 7 May 1934

1931	Arrived	Departed
Boston, Massachusetts	1 July	2 July
Gloucester, Massachusetts	2 July	3 July
Portsmouth, New Hampshire	3 July	12 July
Bar Harbor, Maine	13 July	13 July
Bath, Maine	14 July	17 July
Portland, Maine	17 July	23 July
Gloucester, Massachusetts	23 July	29 July
Marblehead, Massachusetts	29 July	30 July
New Bedford, Massachusetts	31 July	6 August
Providence, Rhode Island	6 August	10 August
Newport, Rhode Island	10 August	13 August
New London, Connecticut	13 August	20 August
Montauk, New York	20 August	25 August
Oyster Bay, New York	25 August	28 August
New York, New York	29 August	14 September
Wilmington, Delaware	16 September	18 September
Philadelphia, Pennsylvania	18 September	1 October
Newport News, Virginia	2 October	9 October
Norfolk, Virginia	9 October	16 October
Yorktown, Virginia	16 October	23 October
Baltimore, Maryland	24 October	2 November
Annapolis, Maryland	2 November	5 November
Quantico, Virginia	6 November	7 November
Washington, D.C.	7 November	18 November
Wilmington, North Carolina	21 November	30 November
Charleston, South Carolina	1 December	6 December
Savannah, Georgia	7 December	11 December
Brunswick, Georgia	12 December	15 December
Jacksonville, Florida	16 December	21 December
Miami, Florida	23 December	30 December

1932	Arrived	Departed
Key West, Florida	31 December, 1931	6 January
Pensacola, Florida	6 January	11 January
Mobile, Alabama	11 January	18 January
Baton Rouge, Louisiana	20 January	27 January
New Orleans, Louisiana	27 January	12 February
Corpus Christie, Texas	14 February	23 February
Galveston, Texas	24 February	25 February
Houston, Texas	25 February	1 March
Galveston, Texas	1 March	7 March
Beaumont, Texas	8 March	12 March
Port Arthur, Texas	12 March	17 March
Orange, Texas	17 March	19 March
Lake Charles, Louisiana	19 March	22 March
Gulfport, Mississippi	25 March	29 March
Port Saint Joe, Florida	30 March	1 April
Tampa, Florida	3 April	7 April
St. Petersburg, Florida	7 April	9 April
Washington, D.C.	16 April	11 May
Alexandria, Virginia	11 May	12 May
Washington, D.C.	23 May	8 December
Guantanamo Bay, Cuba	14 December	19 December
Cristobal, Canal Zone	22 December	27 December

1933	Arrived	Departed
Balboa, Canal Zone	27 December, 1932	7 January
San Diego, California	21 January	16 February
San Pedro, California	17 February	10 March
Long Beach, California	10 March	19 March
Santa Barbara, California	20 March	20 March
(No stop made here due to rough seas)		
San Francisco, California	24 March	12 April
Oakland, California	12 April	26 April
Vallejo, California	26 April	2 May
Astoria, Oregon	6 May	15 May

1933	Arrived	Departed
Grays Harbor, Washington	16 May	26 May
Port Angeles, Washington	27 May	31 May
Seattle, Washington	31 May	15 June
Tacoma, Washington	15 June	22 June
Olympia, Washington	22 June	1 July
Bremerton, Washington	1 July	7 July
Everett, Washington	7 July	14 July
Bellingham, Washington	14 July	20 July
Anacortes, Washington	20 July	26 July
Port Townsend, Washington	26 July	30 July
Astoria, Oregon	31 July	2 August
Portland, Oregon	2 August	22 August
Kalama, Washington	22 August	24 August
Longview, Washington	24 August	28 August
San Francisco, California	2 September	15 September
Oakland, California	15 September	29 September
Santa Cruz, California	29 September	30 September
Monterey, California	30 September	1 October
Port San Luis, California	2 October	2 October
(No stop here due to fog)		
Santa Barbara, California	3 October	4 October
Ventura, California	4 October	5 October
Santa Monica, California	5 October	5 October
Long Beach, California	6 October	19 October
San Pedro, California	19 October	2 November
Avalon, California	2 November	2 November

1934	Arrived	Departed
San Diego, California	3 November, 1933	20 March
Balboa, Canal Zone	2 April	7 April
Cristobal, Canal Zone	7 April	8 April
St. Petersburg, Florida	14 April	23 April
Charleston, South Carolina	23 April	3 May
Boston, Massachusetts	7 May	**End of Tour** [1]

Acknowledgments

I would like to thank Dr. Jennifer Bryan and Mr. David Onofrio of the Special Archives Department, Nimitz Library, U.S. Naval Academy for their assistance in making these scrapbooks and the *Constitution's* Captain's Night Order Book available.

I would also like to thank Ms. Kate Monea, Archivist of the USS Constitution Museum, for her help in accessing the museum's collection.

I would especially like to thank my wife, Mary. Without her support and professional editing, this book would have been a much poorer effort.

Volume 1 - USS *Constitution* Scrapbooks, Nimitz Library

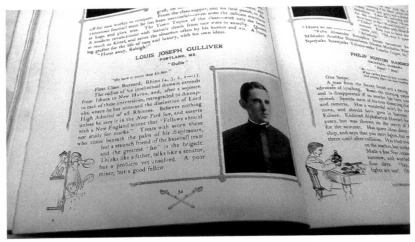

Lucky Bag entry for Louis J. Gulliver, 1907

Sources

Extensive use is made of the official deck logs of the USS *Constitution* and the USS *Grebe* over the period of the cruise. Material from these logs is decribed below.

USS *Grebe* deck logs, National Archives, Record Group 24. Wherever these are referenced, the information comes from those logs on or about the date mentioned.

USS *Constitution* deck logs, National Archives, Record Group 45. Wherever these are referenced, the information comes from those logs on or about the date mentioned.

Other information for this book comes from three large scrapbooks donated to the U. S. Naval Academy by Commander Louis J. Gulliver, USN (retired). Commander Gulliver was the Commander of the U.S. Frigate *Constitution* for her National Tour. These scrapbooks are maintained in the Special Collections Archive of the Nimitz Library at the Naval Academy. The reference is:

USS *Constitution* Scrapbooks MS 281
Special Collections and Archives Dept.
Nimitz Library
U. S. Naval Academy.

Many of the items in these scrapbooks are newspaper clippings not always clearly identified by newspaper and date. Newspaper clipping sources here will be identified as closely as possible, followed by [LJG].

Endnotes

FORWARD

[1] "Riding a Hobby: Collecting Naval Postmarks," Harold P. Faust, US Naval Institute *Proceedings*, September 1934 Vol. 60/9/371.

CHAPTER 1 • THE RESTORATION OF 1927

[1] National Cruise Scrapbook, compiler unknown, pg. 12. USS Constitution Museum Collection, 2007.1.

[2] Martin, Tyrone G., *A Most Fortunate Ship – A Narrative History of Old Ironsides*, Naval Institute Press, Annapolis, Maryland, 1997, pg. 343.

[3] Gulliver, Louis J., "Renaissance of Old Ironsides," *Marine Review*, Vol. 61, July 1931.

[4] Martin, op. cit., pg. 343–349.

[5] "Old Ironsides Again Commissioned in the Navy," *Boston Globe*, July 2, 1931.

CHAPTER 2 • THE CAPTAIN–COMMANDER LOUIS J. GULLIVER

[1] Gulliver, Louis J., USS *Constitution* Scrapbooks, Vol. 3, Nimitz Library, U.S. Naval Academy, Special Collections Archive, MS 281. Scrapbooks of the National tour compiled by Commander Gulliver. Undated newspaper clipping from the *Portland Press* (Maine).

[2] *Lucky Bag*, U.S. Naval Academy Year Book, 1907 Edition, Annapolis, Maryland. Nimitz Library, U.S. Naval Academy.

[3] Joseph Severe Emile Beland's National Cruise Scrapbook, pg. 1. USS Constitution Museum Collection, 1779.1.

[4] shipscribe website, www.shipscribe.com/usnaux/AC/AC11.html.

[5] "Old Ironsides Acclaimed," *Los Angeles Times*, June 25, 1933.

[6] Gulliver, Louis J., USS *Constitution* Scrapbooks, Vol. 1. Personal letter from Admiral Hart.

[7] Gulliver, Louis J., USS *Constitution* Scrapbooks, Vol. 1, Naval Message orders. Martin, in *A Most Fortunate Ship – A Narrative History of Old Ironsides* gives the date of Gulliver's orders as March 14, 1931. These may have been a modified set from the one in Commander Gulliver's Scrapbook.

[8] USS Constitution Museum Website, "Captains of Constitution," www.usscm.org.

[9] Gulliver, Louis J., "Gulliver's Travels —The Cruise of the U.S.F. Constitution," *Leatherneck*, June 1938.

[10] "High Praise Given Police By Hartley," *Los Angeles Times*, February 21, 1933.

[11] "Old Ironsides Robbed of 24lb Cannon Ball," *Boston Globe*, 20 February, 1933.

[12] Gulliver, Louis J., USS *Constitution* Scrapbooks, Vol. 1, Nimitz Library, U.S. Naval Academy, Special Collections Archive–MS 281. Scrapbooks of the National tour compiled by Commander Gulliver, letter from Mary Gail Gulliver.

CHAPTER 3 • OFFICERS AND CREW

[1] Williams, Dion, "Old Ironsides," *Marine Corps Gazette*, August, 1931.

[2] Henry Galaske's National Cruise Scrapbook, pg. 38. USS Constitution Museum Collection, 1854.1.

[3] USS *Constitution* Deck Logs, National Archives, Record Group 45.

[4] James William Tytler's National Cruise Scrapbook, 1931–1934, pg.50. USS Constitution Museum Collection, 1870.1a,b.

[5] USS *Constitution* Deck Logs, op.cit.

[6] USS *Grebe* Deck logs, National Archives, Record Group 24.

[7] Gulliver, Louis J. "Gulliver's Travels," *Leatherneck*, June 1938.

[8] Ibid.

CHAPTER 4 • USS GREBE – FAITHFUL SERVANT TO OLD IRONSIDES

[1] *Dictionary of American Naval Fighting Ships* (DANFS) – Naval History and Heritage command. http://www.history.navy.mil/research/histories/ship-histories/danfs/g/grebe.html.

[2] "A Mind of Her Own," Charles F. Adams, U.S. Naval Institute *Proceedings*, July 1997 Vol. 123/7/1,133.

[3] USS *Grebe* Deck logs, National Archives, Record Group 24.

[4] "A Mind of Her Own," Charles F. Adams, U.S. Naval Institute *Proceedings*, July 1997 Vol. 123/7/1,133.

[5] USS *Constitution* Deck Logs, National Archives, Record Group 45.

[6] USS *Grebe* Deck logs, op.cit.

[7] Gulliver, Louis J., *Captain's Night Order Book*, USS *Constitution*, 2 July 1931 – 8 May 1934, MS 115, Special Collections and Archives Dept., Nimitz Library, U. S. Naval Academy.

[8] *Orange Leader* (California), March 17, 1932 [LJG].

[9] USS *Grebe* Deck logs, op.cit.

[10] *A Most Fortunate Ship – A Narrative History of Old Ironsides* – Tyrone G. Martin, Naval Institute Press, Annapolis, Maryland, 1997, pg. 352.

[11] *Long Beach Free Press*, October 12, 1933 [LJG].

[12] *San Diego Union*, November 14, 1933 [LJG].

[13] Franciezek "Frank" Prusz's National Cruise Scrapbook, 1931–1934, pg. 26. USS Constitution Museum Collection, 1869.1. The bear's name was variously reported as "Scrappy" and "Crappy." Based on the author's experience with sailors and what he knows about bears, the latter was probably preferred, at least at sea.

[14] USS *Constitution* Scrapbook, Vol. 3.

[15] Martin, op. cit. pg. 354-355.

[16] USS *Constitution* Deck Logs, op.cit.

[17] USS *Constitution* Captain's Night Order Book, op. cit.

[18] Naval Message form, USS *Constitution* Scrapbook,Vol. 3 [LJG].

[19] DANFS, op. cit.

CHAPTER 5 • THE TOUR

[1] Gulliver, Louis J. USS *Constitution* Scrapbooks, 1931–1934, Vol.1, scrapbooks compiled by Commander Gulliver. Special Collections Archive, Nimitz Library, U.S. Naval Academy, MS 281, personal letter from Mr. Wood.

[2] Ibid., broadcast script.

[3] "6564 More View Old Frigate in Portsmouth," *Boston Globe*, July 8. 1931.

[4] USS *Constitution* Deck Logs, National Archives, Record Group 45.

[5] "Old Ironsides Reaches Bath, ME," *Boston Globe*, July 15, 1931.

[6] USS *Constitution* Deck Logs, op.cit.

[7] "Marblehead to Entertain Officers on Constitution," *Boston Globe*, July 27, 1931.

[8] USS *Constitution* Deck Logs, op.cit.

[9] Ibid.

[10] "New York Greets Old Ironsides," *Boston Globe*, August 30, 1931.

[11] USS *Constitution* Deck Logs, op.cit.

[12] "Old Ironsides Slated to Visit Philadelphia," *Boston Globe*, August 22, 1931.

[13] USS *Constitution* Deck Logs, op.cit.

[14] Martin, Tyrone G., *A Most Fortunate Ship – A Narrative History of Old Ironsides*, Naval Institute Press, 1997, pg. 351.

[15] USS *Constitution* Deck Logs, op.cit.

[16] "Veterans Rap Adams for Navy Yard Note," *Boston Globe*, October 27, 1931.

[17] "McCormack Raps Docking of Frigate at Capital," *Boston Globe*, November 11, 1931. "Hoover Inspects Historic Frigate," *Boston Globe*, Nov. 11, 1931. "Old Ironsides to Resume Cruise," *Boston Globe*, Nov. 17, 1931.

[18] "Annapolis Visited by Old Ironsides," *Washington Post*, Nov. 3, 1931.

[19] USS *Constitution* Deck Logs, op.cit.

[20] Ibid.

[21] Gulliver, Louis J., USS *Constitution* Scrapbooks, 1931–1934, Vol. 1, scrapbooks compiled by Commander Gulliver, Special Collections Archive, Nimitz Library, U.S. Naval Academy, MS 281, personal letter to Commander Gulliver.

[22] USS *Constitution* Deck Logs, op.cit.

[23] "Navy Asks Probe of Publicity Agent," *Washington Post*, December 19, 1931.

[24] USS *Constitution* Deck Logs, op.cit.

[25] Ibid.

[26] Martin, Tyrone G., *A Most Fortunate Ship – A Narrative History of Old Ironsides*, Naval Institute Press, 1997, pg. 352–353.

[27] Gulliver, Louis J. USS *Constitution* Scrapbooks, op.cit., letter from Tampa customs office, dated May 16, 1932.

[28] Ibid., *Galveston Tribune*, February 24, 1932.

[29] USS *Grebe* Deck logs, National Archives, Record Group 24.

[30] "Old Salt Has Rendezvous with His Old Ironsides," *Boston Globe*, April 8, 1932.

[31] Martin, Tyrone G., op. cit., pg. 353.

[32] USS *Constitution* Deck Logs, op.cit.

[33] "Sightless Today Visit USS Constitution," *Washington Post*, April 18, 1932.

[34] "Old Ironsides Is Set Adrift by High Winds," *Washington Post*, May 13, 1932.

[35] USS *Constitution* Deck Logs, op.cit.

[36] USS *Grebe* Deck logs, National Archives, Record Group 24.

[37] USS *Constitution* Deck Logs, op.cit.

[38] U.S. Militaria Forum. http://www.usmilitariaforum.com/forums/index.php?/topic/142181-rear-admiral-henry-hartley/. Military Times Hall of Valor. http://valor.militarytimes.com/recipient.php?recipientid=19556.

[39] "Baby Squirms and Chuckles During Christening on Ship," *Washington Post*, June 27, 1932.

[40] Martin, Tyrone G., *A Most Fortunate Ship – A Narrative History of Old Ironsides*, Naval Institute Press, 1997, pg. 353.

[41] USS *Grebe* Deck logs, op.cit.

[42] USS *Constitution* Deck Logs, op.cit.

[43] Ibid.

[44] Ibid.

[45] Ibid.

[46] "British Board Old Ironsides," *Boston Globe*, November 20, 1932.

[47] USS *Constitution* Deck Logs, op.cit.

[48] Ibid.

[49] USS *Grebe* Deck logs, op.cit.

[50] Martin, Tyrone G., op. cit., pg. 354.

[51] "San Diego Greets Constitution," *Los Angeles Times*, January 22, 1933.

[52] Joseph Severe Emile Beland's National Cruise Scrapbook, pg. 6. USS Constitution Museum Collection, 1779.1.

[53] USS *Constitution* Deck Logs, op.cit.

[54] Gulliver, Louis J., USS *Constitution* Scrapbooks, op.cit., personal letter to Commander Gulliver, dated February 10, 1933.

[55] "Went 900 Miles to See Constitution," *Boston Globe*, April 20, 1934.

[56] "Old Ironsides Breaks Record," *Los Angeles Times*, Feb. 25, 1933.

[57] USS *Constitution* Deck Logs, op.cit.

[58] Martin, Tyrone G., op. cit., pg. 355.

[59] Gulliver Scrapbooks, Vol. 2, "Frigate Makes Jobs for Idle," *San Pedro News Pilot*, February 21, 1933.

[60] "Cities Plan Excursions to See Old Ironsides," *Los Angeles Times*, February 15, 1933. "Santa Monica Schools to Visit Frigate Friday," *Los Angeles Times*, February 22, 1933. "Let's Help Every Child See Old Ironsides," *Los Angeles Times*, February 23, 1933.

[61] "Children First in Frigate Visit," *Los Angeles Times*, March 1, 1933.

[62] "Old Ironsides Time Extended," *Los Angeles Times*, March 7, 1933.

[63] California Department of Conservation. http://www. conservation.ca.gov/cgs/News/pages/longbeach.aspx.

[64] Letter from Captain Louis J. Gulliver to Charles F. Wettach, April 28, 1933. USS Constitution Museum Collection, 1063.1.

[65] USS *Grebe* Deck logs, National Archives, Record Group 24.

[66] USS *Constitution* Deck Logs, National Archives, Record Group 45.

[67] Gulliver, Louis J., USS *Constitution* Scrapbooks, op.cit., Newspaper clipping dated March 30, 1933.

[68] USS *Constitution* Deck Logs, op.cit.

[69] "Search For Bomb on Old Ironsides," *Boston Globe*, April 8, 1933.

[70] USS *Grebe* Deck Logs, op.cit.

[71] USS *Constitution* Deck Logs, op.cit.

[72] Joseph Severe Emile Beland's National Cruise Scrapbook, pg. 24. USS Constitution Museum Collection, 1779.1. Notes added by the museum identify the date of the clipping as August 6, 1933 and indicate the incident caused the cancellation of a return visit to Astoria, but the tour itinerary published by the museum indicates that the ship was in Astoria again July 31 and August 2, 1933.

[73] USS *Constitution* Deck Logs, op.cit.

[74] Ibid.

[75] "For Some, Constitution's Visit Left Scars, Memories," *Anacortes American*, August 13, 1997.

[76] "Pictures of the Past," Anacortes American, July 30, 1997.

[77] National Cruise Scrapbook, compiler unknown. USS Constitution Museum Collection, 2007.1.

[78] USS *Constitution* Deck Logs, op.cit.

[79] Ibid.

[80] Ibid.

[81] Ibid.

[82] "Old Ironsides to Stay at San Diego Till March," *Los Angeles Times*, November 16, 1933.

[83] USS *Constitution* Deck Logs, op.cit.

[84] "Grace W. Gulliver, Daughter of Captain, Weds Lieut Thompson on Deck of Historic Constitution," *Boston Globe*, March 18, 1934, USS Constitution Museum, Scrapbook compiled by Joseph S. E. Bland. "After Wedding Aboard Constitution," undated newspaper clipping from the *Portland Press* (Maine), pg. 4.

[85] Gulliver, Louis J., USS *Constitution* Scrapbooks, 1931–1934, Vol. 2, op.cit., newspaper clipping "Skipper's Wife and Children Will Join Crew for Six Month's Cruise," *Long Beach Press Telegram*, March 10, 1933.

[86] Gulliver, Louis J., USS *Constitution* Scrapbooks, 1931–1934, Vol. 3,op.cit., unidentified and undated newspaper clipping.

[87] USS *Constitution* Deck Logs, op.cit.

[88] Ibid.

[89] USS *Grebe* Deck Logs, op.cit.

[90] Gulliver, Louis J., USS *Constitution, Captain's Night Orders*, Special Collections Archive, Nimitz Library, U.S. Naval Academy, MS 115.

[91] USS *Constitution* Deck Logs, op.cit.

[92] "Ironsides May Sail Under Own Canvas," *Boston Globe*, April 28, 1934.

CHAPTER 6 • TOUR ROUTINES

[1] Gulliver, Louis J., USS *Constitution, Captain's Night Order Book*, U.S. Naval Academy, Nimitz Library, Special Collections Archive, MS 115.

[2] Gulliver, Louis J. "Gulliver's Travels," *Leatherneck*, June 1938.

[3] USS *Constitution* Deck Logs, op.cit.

[4] "Crowd Marvels at Skill of Modern Gobs in Handling Sails," *Washington Post*, July 20, 1932.

[5] Gulliver, Louis J., USS Constitution National Tour scrapbooks, U.S. Naval Academy, Nimitz Library, Special Collections Archive, MS 281, Clipping from *Our Navy*, Mid December, 1934.

[6] Gulliver, Louis J. "Gulliver's Travels" *Leatherneck*, June 1938.

CHAPTER 7 • THE NAVAL POSTMARK COLLECTORS

[1] Navy Postal Clerk Association web site. http:// navypostalclerkassoc.org/?page_id = 2498.

[2] Faust, Harold P. "Riding a Hobby: Collecting Naval Postmarks," U.S. Naval Institute *Proceedings*, September 1934.

[3] Universal Ship Cancellation Society. http://www.uscs.org/ about-uscs/history-of-uscs/.

[4] Gulliver, Louis J., USS *Constitution* National Tour Scrapbooks, Vol.1, U. S. Naval Academy, Nimitz Library, Special Collections Archive, MS 281, clipping from *Our Navy* magazine.

[5] Gulliver, Louis J., USS *Constitution* National Tour Scrapbooks, Volume 2, U.S. Naval Academy, Nimitz Library, Special Collections Archive, MS 281. "Little Post Office on Frigate One of Busiest" clipping from *Portland Morning Oregonian* dated August 8, 1933.

[6] Gulliver, Louis J., USS *Constitution* National Tour Scrapbooks, Vol. 2, U. S. Naval Academy, Nimitz Library, Special Collections Archive, MS 281, "Thousands of Letters Get Cachet Stamp" clipping from *Long View Daily News*, dated August 24,1933.

[7] Navy Postal Clerk Association. http://navypostalclerkassoc. org/?page_id = 2498.

EPILOGUE

[1] Gulliver, Louis J., USS *Constitution* National Tour Scrapbooks, Vol. 2, U.S. Naval Academy, Nimitz Library, Special Collections Archive, MS 281, "Sweetheart of Sailors Chosen," newspaper clipping, *Port Angeles News*, May 27, 1933.

[2] Gulliver, Louis J., USS *Constitution* National Tour Scrapbooks Vol. 3, U. S. Naval Academy, Nimitz Library, Special Collections Archive, MS 281, Unidentified and undated newspaper clipping.

[3] Gulliver, Louis J., "Gulliver's Travels," *Leatherneck*, June 1938.

[4] Gulliver, Louis J., USS *Constitution* National Tour Scrapbooks, Vol. 3, U. S. Naval Academy, Nimitz Library, Special Collections Archive, MS 281, Personal letter from Admiral Sellers, September 23, 1933.

[5] Gulliver, Louis J., USS *Constitution* National Tour Scrapbooks, Vol. 3, U.S. Naval Academy, Nimitz Library, Special Collections Archive, MS 281, Personal letters, orders and newspaper clippings as indicated.

[6] Naval Academy Alumni Association member jacket for Louis J. Gulliver, U.S. Naval Academy, Nimitz Library.

APPENDIX I

HISTORY AND TECHNICAL CHARACTERISTICS OF THE USS GREBE

[1] navsource.org, Naval history archive. http://www.navsource.org/archives/11/02043.html.

APPENDIX II

TOUR ITINERARY

[1] "Ports Visited During USS Constitution's 1931–1934 National Cruise." Courtesy USS Constitution Museum.

About the Author

PHILLIP PARKER was raised in Bozeman, Montana, and received an appointment to the U.S. Naval Academy from Senator Mike Mansfield. He graduated from the Naval Academy in 1971 and served aboard USS *Simon Bolivar* (SSBN 641) as an engineering division officer and at the Nuclear Power Training Unit, Ballston Spa, New York, as an instructor and section leader. Following his Naval service he earned a Master's Degree in Computer Science from the Johns Hopkins University and worked in that field in the Washington, D.C. area, including more than 30 years supporting NASA at the Goddard Space Flight Center through Orbital-ATK. He supported several missions at Goddard, including the Hubble Space Telescope, Earth Observing System, AQUA, TERRA and James Webb Space Telescope. He is retired and lives in Billings, Montana.

Constitution, by Michele Felice Corné, c. 1803.
Courtesy of the USS Constitution Museum. Naval History & Heritage Command Detachment Boston Loan.